HOW TO TRANSFORM YOUR LIFE AND BE PROSPEROUS

(Easy steps to turning your talents into prosperity)

BY JANET MELWANI

YES, you have what it takes to start your assignment in life!
Let's birth it together and remember…

With GOD ALL things are possible!

Scripture quotations are from the King James Version of the Holy Bible unless otherwise indicated.

ISBN: ISBN-13: 978-1517588618

Published by: God Wills Ministry

Prayer

Father God, I come to You with thanksgiving and praise. I thank You for all You have done in my life and all that You are about to do. I acknowledge You as my Savior, Provider, Healer, Protector and my All In All.

As I step out in faith to do what You have called me to do, I ask for Your guidance, knowledge, wisdom, understanding, grace, protection, divine connections and divine favor.

I thank You in advance as I glorify You in Jesus' name, Amen.

Thank You, Jesus! Thank You, Lord! Thank You, Holy Spirit!

Dedication

To my awesome and anointed husband Eric Melwani, I welcome my new chapter with you. I look forward to what God has in store for us.

To my amazing children, Dejohn, Tevano, Geovano Green, and their spouses, your labor of love towards this project has been amazing. Yes, as you always say, "When mom starts a project that means we start it too." As I delegated to you the different "behind the scene" responsibilities of this project, you never complained; instead, you carried out the different tasks with excellence. Thanks for helping to make this project what it is. I love you all.

Objectives

- Learning the importance of putting God first in everything you do
- Developing a more mature and spiritual "You"
- Listening to God's voice for direction
- Developing your physical being
- Disconnecting from destiny killers and negative people
- Connecting with positive business-minded and ministry-minded people
- Understanding the concept and the importance of tithing both talents and finances
- Communicating your dreams of owning your own business with your significant other or immediate family members
- Learning how to build your business and protect your blessings from God
- Selecting a mentor and a prayer partner
- The importance of having a prayer life
- The importance of praising and worshiping God
- Why we should we pay attention to our dreams and visions
- How we walk in the supernatural power of God
- Why it is important to apply faith to our everyday situations

- God is giving us directions in our dreams and visions for our ministries, businesses, careers and family
- How to get the interpretation of our dreams and visions
- The three stages of life and what to do as we are faced with them in our careers, businesses or ministries
- Learning the fundamentals of starting your own business
- Writing your business plan
- The importance of business networking/building a relationship with people within your community
- Determining the legal structure of your business/ministry
- Registering your business/ministry
- Choosing your business/ministry location
- How to market your goods and services
- Selecting appropriate social media for the growth of your business/ministry
- Selecting and retaining the most qualified workforce at an optimum performance level
- Learning the responsibilities of being an employer
- Preparing your start-up expense worksheet
- Staying faithful to your dream
- 100+ prayer points

Table of Contents

- **Chapter One (Section 1)**
- **The Foundation of a Successful Business, Ministry and Personal Venture**
  - Mental
    - Renewing Your Mind for the Manifestation of God's Will for Your Life
    - Life and Death is in the Power of Our Tongue
  - Physical
    - Physical Preparation on How to Maximize Prosperity
  - Spiritual
    - Strengthen Your Spiritual Relationship with God
    - Developing a More Intimate Relationship with God Through Thanksgiving, Praise, Worship, Praying, Fasting, and Meditating on the Word of God
    - How to Walk in the Supernatural Provision of God
    - Some Supernatural Ways of God in My Life
    - How to Hear the Voice of God
    - Some Things that We Can Do to Magnify the Presence of God in Our Life
  - Applying Faith to God's Will for Your Life is Crucial
    - What is Faith?

- How Important is Faith to God?
- Faith Declarations
- Tithes and Offering
- Eight Keys to a Prosperous Life
- Call to Action Excercise Exercise
- Chapter Assignment

- **Chapter Two**
- **Personal Development**
- My Time Spent Per 24 Hours Exercise
- Unforgiveness
- What Does Our Bible Say About Unforgiveness
- Daily Declaration Scriptures
- God Can Use Us if We Submit to Him
- Chapter Assignment

- **Chapter Three**
- **Staying Faithful to God Through All Stages of Life**
- Season One: Instantaneous Blessings
- Season One Action: What Do You Do?
- Season Two: Am I Suffering or Am I Reaping?
- Season Two Action: What Do You Do?

- Season Three: Promotion/New Beginning
- Season Three Action: What do you do?
- Some Common Spiritual Road Blocks that Cause Failure in Life
    - Daily Check Point for God to Manifest More in Our Life
    - Prayer Points for Success
    - My Time Spent Per 24 Hours 2nd Exercise
- **Chapter Four**
- **God Speaks to Us Through Dreams and Visions**
    - What is a Vision?
    - What is a Dream?
    - How to Strengthen Your Communication with God Through Dreams and Visions
    - Reasons Why We Should Pay Attention to Our Dreams and Visions
    - Two Types of Dreams
        - Dreams About Us
        - Dreams About Others
    - Ways in Which God Helps Us to Understand Our Dreams
    - Some Basic Principles for Interpreting Dreams

- Symbols in Our Dreams
- Important Things About Dreams and Visions
- Visions
  - Visions Come as a Turning Point in Our Life
  - Five Keys for Your Visions to Manifest
  - Call to Action Excercise Exercise

◦ **Chapter Five**

◦ **Transitioning Into Who You are Created to Be**

- New Venture Test
- Call to Action Excercise Exercise
- Final Section Prayer
- Salvation Prayer

◦ **Chapter Six (Section 2)**

◦ **Business Plan Outline**

- Writing Your Business Plan
- Sample Business Plan
  - Components of a Business Plan
  - Company Description
  - Industry Analysis
  - Services and Products

    - Target Market
    - Marketing Plan and Strategy
    - Operations
    - Management and Organization
  - Chapter Assignment
- **Chapter Seven**
- **Formulating Your Business**
  - Determining the Legal Structure of Your Business
  - Registering Your Business
  - Chapter Assignment
- **Chapter Eight**
- **How to Choose Your Business Location**
  - Chapter Assignment
- **Chapter Nine**
- **Positioning Your Business for Success**
  - Advertising and Marketing
  - Creating Your Business Card and Flyer
  - Social Media
  - Chapter Assignment
- **Chapter Ten**

- **Selecting a Successful Team**
  - Making the Right Hiring Decisions
  - Maintaining Your Workforce
  - Employer Responsibility
  - Chapter Assignment
- **Chapter Eleven**
- **Accounting**
  - Chapter Assignment
- **Chapter Twelve**
- **Successful Networking**
  - Getting Prepared for a Networking Event
  - Chapter Assignment
- **Summary Chapter**
- **Stay Encouraged**
  - Build Your Network Group

About the Author

Janet worked over twenty years in the hospitality industry. She started her career at a five-star hotel in New York City as a PBX operator. After working six months in her position, she was promoted to PBX supervisor where she supervised thirty-two operators. Even though she was the youngest staff member and had the fewest years of experience in her department, Janet did not let all the negative and spiteful words from her coworkers kill her enthusiasm. Instead, she used it as fuel to keep her fire burning. Within three months in her position, she was able to gain the respect and loyalty from her staff. Three years later, she was promoted to front office supervisor. Janet became bored in this position so she decided to transfer to the accounting department where she received numerous awards, including Associate of the Year. As if this did not keep her busy enough, she took on some of the human resources department responsibilities such as planning the annual associate picnic and holiday party for their four hundred-plus associates. Janet's general manger saw great potential in her as a director of human resources and encouraged her to start a career in Human Resources (HR). She was then transferred to Human Resources where she spent the next two years learning all the disciplines in that field (recruiting, employee relations, employee benefits and payroll) and volunteering on special HR projects. She was then transferred to another state as a human resources manager and one year later, she became the director of human resources.

As a dedicated and hardworking professional, she managed to maintain high associate satisfaction, reducing the amount of associates leaving the company as she maximized and promoted talents around her. Her love for her associates went beyond her call of duty as she supported their family successes and grieved with them during their times of distress or loss of family members.

As busy as she was as a director of human resources, Janet consistently exemplified the importance of giving back to the community. In one year, she was able to accomplish the following:

- Fed 1767 homeless men and children
- Collected over 100 cellular phones for the Secure A Call Foundation
- Collected over 65 pairs of old eye glasses for donations
- Collected over 112 pairs of old sneakers to refurbish tennis courts
- Raised funds for the Children's Miracle Network
- Planned and successfully executed a hotel market picnic for over 3,000 associates and families

In July of 2009, Janet experienced the worst year of her professional career. At that time, she began to strengthen her relationship with God through prayer and fasting. One day, she prayed and asked God to close all doors that needed to be closed and to open all doors that needed to be opened in her life. Fewer than forthy eight hours later, Janet noticed what she described as everything in my life became chaotic. First, her career as director of human resources ended abruptly and twenty four hours after that, her fiancé called and ended their relationship of three years. Janet then turned to God for answers as to why it seemed that everything was going wrong in her life, and then she remembered how good God is and immediately began to thank Him for her life and the lives of her sons. On the third night of this turn of events, God told to Janet in a dream, "You prayed for me to close all doors that needed to be closed and to open all doors that needed to be opened, and I answered your prayer." From that day forth, Janet was at peace with everything that was happening in her life.

Janet then decided it was time for her to start her own business. Even though it was no secret in her family that she was a gifted cook and had the wits of a tough business woman, they all were disappointed that she would no longer do what she does best, which was taking care of others and defending the voiceless as a director of human resources.

In 2010, Janet communicated with her pastor and two ministers at her home church the importance and benefit of a having a business ministry in the church. Janet was able to convince them all of this project; the only problem was that they wanted her to head this ministry and she without a doubt stated, No, I am only here to make the suggestion and support." She also stated that she had another to business focus on and that was her priority.

A few weeks after the meeting with her church leaders, Janet got a vision from God to head the Entrepreneur/Business Ministry at her home church. She tried to negotiate with God by telling Him she could do a better job of helping the ministry and not leading it; but when God reminded her of the story of Jonah, she surrendered. Janet then fasted and prayed for God's direction as she started to put together the material she would be teaching from, and it became the book you are now reading. Janet started the first entrepreneur class, "How to Start Your Business" in April of 2010 with forthy students.

As if that did not keep her busy enough, this young single mom continued to mentor her three sons, Dejohn, Tevano, and Geovano Green who are now married, as well as her first grandchild Dejohn Jr Malachi. She often says that her first love is God and her second love is her three sons.

Author's Acknowledgements

Dr. Robert Spooney, former President of the African American Chamber of Commerce of Central Florida, I am so grateful to you for teaching the students how to sell their businesses and the positive words you have imparted in their lives. Pamela Martin, former office manager for the Chamber, we appreciate all your support. Mr. Errick Young, former manager for Orange County Business Development, the time you spent connecting these new business owners to seasoned business owners and mentoring and guiding them as they entered the world of business is greatly appreciated. Lady D, Host of Caribbean Connection, WOKB Radio 1680 AM and TV talk show host, I love you and appreciate all the air time you have given to this ministry, and the time you have spent emceeing our networking events.

I am so grateful to all the business owners who have taken this class and have successfully started your own businesses. I thank you for confirming that this class is needed in our church and community. Your testimonies of God's divine favor and divine connections validate that God is leading this ministry to great success.

To my incredible sister, Priscilla Blair and brother-in-law Charles Blair, thanks for always having my back, loving me unconditionally and believing in this vision God has on my life. Even when it doesn't make sense to you, you support me. Your positive words of encouragement are priceless. I love you both!

Finally, to Sydney Rowe, my uncle, one of my prayer warriors and a mighty man of God, thanks for listening to me, praying with me and guiding me biblically throughout this journey. I love you, and may God continue to richly bless you and your ministry.

Preface

This book was written for everyone who wants to start their own business, ministry or further their career. There is no age limit, no culture limit, no gender limit, no educational limit and no denominational limit. In other words, if you are breathing and want to start your own business, ministry or career, this book was written for you. I prayed and fasted prior to writing this book. I have asked God to speak to the hearts of His people and let them know that it's through divine favor and divine appointment that they have purchased this book or was blessed with this book. I prayed to God that He would give each of you visions of confirmation that this is your season of new beginning. God let me know that you are going through a season that is signaling it's time for you to make changes in your life. This is your new season; embrace it, be bold and step out in faith to do what God has pleased in your heart. Let's embrace it positively. Let's seek God's guidance and a closer relationship with Him as He guides us to another level. Let's come together and unite as God's children doing Kingdom business. Let's help each other. Let's support each other. And finally, let's love each other the way God intended.

Remember that God has already equipped us with the tools we need to make the first move: There are three sections in this book. First section deals with personal developemen, renewing of our mind and building a closer relationship with God. Section two deals with the fudemental of starting a business or ministry, and section three deales with encouraging you to stay focus through the challenging time of your life.

Deuteronomy 8:18 [18]But thou shalt remember the LORD thy God: for it is he that giveth thee power to get wealth that he may establish his covenant which he sware unto thy fathers, as it is this day.

Psalm 37:4 [4]Delight thyself also in the LORD: and he shall give thee the desires of thine heart.

Isaiah 1:19 [19]If ye be willing and obedient, ye shall eat the good of the land.

Pray and ask God to let you know what His will for your life is. Remember, God's will for our lives is always best. Submit yourself to God and ask for His grace and guidance as you start your new journey. It is imperative that you maintain a relationship with God, surround yourself with positive people, sow financial seeds and sow your talents. Be focused and believe in your dream. And most of all, have faith and believe God.

If you apply all of the principles in this book, you will be successful in whatever business, ministry or career you start. Do not focus on where you are but look towards your goal. You cannot run a race looking backwards; it will delay or distract you or even worse, cause an accident. You have to position yourself by looking forward and moving forward. Surround yourself with positive people.

Each and every one of us has at least one gift and talent from God. Ephesians 4:7-8 [7]But unto every one of us is given grace according to the measure of the gift of Christ. [8]Wherefore he saith, When he ascended up on high, he led captivity captive, and gave gifts unto men.

We are living in a supernatural season and God wants to do supernatural things for us. This book will help you position yourself, business and ministry for the supernatural blessings of God.

God is speaking to us through dreams and visions; we have to pay attention to what He is saying. He will give us inventive ideas, directional ideas and information we will need to complete His will for our live. For those of you who believe that God is not speaking to you through dreams and visions, I will teach you some things to do to activate that relationship with Him and how to recognize when He is interpreting our dreams.

Be sure to leverage what you have for what you need. We always have the tools we need to start the ideas God has placed in our hearts.

May God bless you and guide you as you pursue your business, ministry and career ventures He has placed in your heart. You can do it!!! It's within you!!!

Section 1

Chapter One

The Foundation of a Successful Business, Ministry and Personal Venture

When building a house, primarily the first stages are putting the image you visualize the building to look like on paper (blueprint), then presenting your request to get the permit for laying the foundation. The higher and bigger the building, the deeper the pillar should be in the ground to withstand the weight and pressure of the building. If the foundation is not strong enough when wind, storm and hurricane (problems) come, the building will easily be destroyed. Therefore, this chapter will help you build a solid foundation for your ministry, business or career that will be able to withstand the storms of life.

We will discuss the four pillars for a setting a solid foundation for a successful business, ministry or career which are Tithing, Spirituality, and Mental and Physical well-being. Each pillar is very unique yet is dependent of the others for supporting the infrastructure of your business, ministry or career. In other words, you need all four pillars to be a successful business owner and minister. Some areas you might be strong in and others you might be weak in; that's ok, I am here to coach and support you as to how you can balance all four pillars. Also, don't be afraid, intimidated or insecure to use people God has sent to help you, your business or your ministry. Because you are in relationship with God, you will have a discernment of who comes from God to help you or who is on assignment from the devil to abort your destiny.

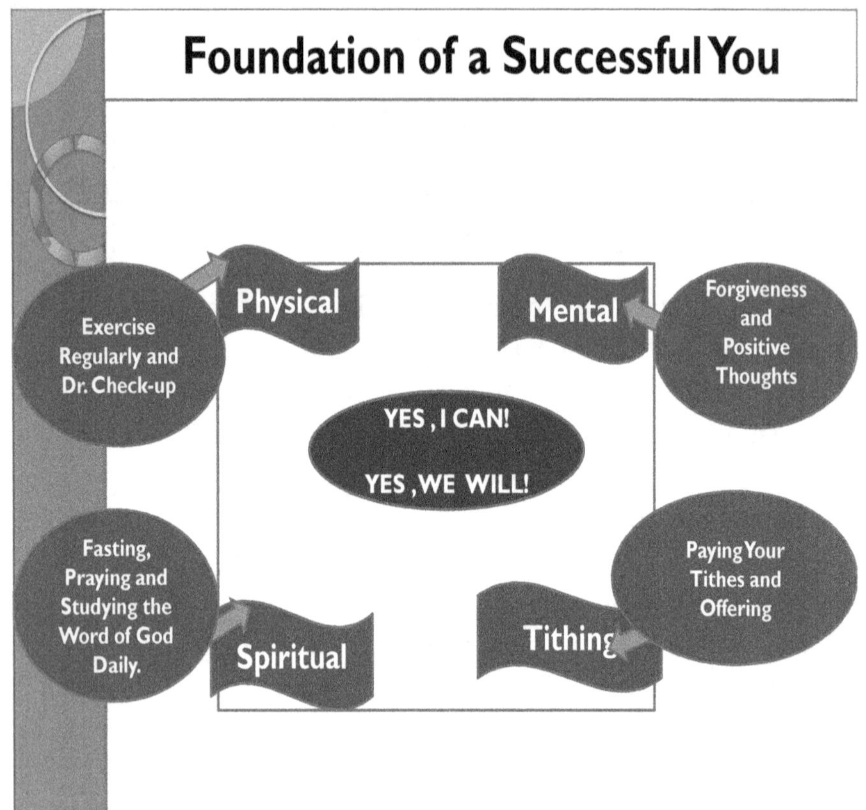

Mental

Renewing Your Mind for the Manifestation of God's Will for Your Life

You create with your mind, Joshua 6: 1-2 KJV [1]Now Jericho was straitly shut up because of the children of Israel: none went out, and none came in. [2]And the LORD said unto Joshua, **See**, I have given into thine hand Jericho, and the king thereof, *and* the mighty men of valour.

You have to imagine it, visualize it, before it can manifest in your life, so see yourself as the successful business owner or ministry leader you desire to build. You cannot go where your mind has not been. The power is within you to create what you want to be. All of your miracles are within your spirit. If you don't choose your imagination, Satan will choose it for you. Romans 12:2 KJV [2]And be not conformed to this world: but be ye transformed by the renewing of your mind, that ye may prove what *is* that good, and acceptable, and perfect, will of God. Reject every negative thought, Proverbs 23:7 KJV [7]For as he thinketh in his heart, so *is* he: Eat and drink, saith he to thee; but his heart *is* not with thee. Whatever you meditate on will become you. Think on this: you body does not go anywhere without your head. Meaning, wherever your mind takes you, that's where you will go.

Mediate on the word of God and you shall have good success. Joshua 1:8 [8]This book of the law shall not depart out of thy mouth; but thou shalt meditate therein day and night, that thou mayest observe to do according to all that is written therein: for then thou shalt make thy way prosperous, and then thou shalt have good success.

Start on purpose to paint the pictures you want to see manifest in your life. Your imagination is your primary creative ability. Whatever you believe will follow you. Whatever you speak about, your mind will gravitate to it. Your words and your thoughts should be in alignment. For example, you should not be building a business and saying: "I am not good at managing this business and my business is going to fail," "I don't have any customers or clients," or "I am not making a profit." Remember, Proverbs 18:21 KJV Death and life *are* in the power of the tongue: and they that love it shall eat the fruit thereof. Whatever you speak over your situation or life will manifest. It's important for us to choose our words wisely.

Life and Death is in the Power of Our Tongue

Try this exercise with me: Think about numbers, count from 1-100 in your mind and at the same time begin to speak the letters of the alphabet, A, B,C,D,E,F,G,H,I,J,K,L,M,N,O,P,Q,R,S,T,U,V,W,X,Y,Z. Now which outpowered the other? Was it your thoughts or your words? If you have done it correctly, the words from your lips should outpower your thoughts. Life and death is in the power of your tongue. STOP SPEAKING NEGATIVE WORDS OVER YOUR LIFE AND YOUR SITUATIONS.

Watch what you meditate upon because your thoughts become language. Your language becomes your actions. Your actions become your habits. Your habits become your character. And your character becomes your destiny. When you speak, you are sowing seeds that you will harvest. It's up to you to make your harvest a good one by sowing positive words. Rather than speaking negative words, sowing seeds of failure and destruction, speak positive words over your situations and expect a positive harvest.

Jesus told us in Mark 12:28-30 KJV [28]And one of the scribes came, and having heard them reasoning together, and perceiving that he had answered them well, asked him, Which is the first commandment of all? [29]And Jesus answered him, The first of all the commandments *is*, Hear, O Israel; The Lord our God is one Lord: [30]And thou shalt love the Lord thy God with all thy heart, and with all thy soul, and ***with all thy mind***, and with all thy strength: this *is* the first. Whatever we meditate upon, we will begin to verbalize and later it will manifest in our lives. Therefore, we have to guard our thoughts. We have to be deliberate to think upon that which we desire to manifest in our life.

Physical

Physical Preparation on How to Maximize Prosperity

There are too many people who start and operate businesses that have not been able to reap the true harvest from their businesses only because they neglect their health during the process and as a result, they die untimely an death. They were not able to reap the harvest and enjoy their blessings from God. It is important for us to have a balanced life. Yes, we can discipline ourselves to do so. Build, live and enjoy life.

1 Corinthians 6:19

19What? know ye not that your body is the temple of the Holy Ghost *which is* in you, which ye have of God, and ye are not your own?

2 Corinthians 6:16-17

16And what agreement hath the temple of God with idols? for ye
are the temple of the living God; as God hath said, I will dwell in
them, and walk in *them*; and I will be their God, and they shall be
my people. 17Wherefore come out from among them, and be ye
separate, saith the Lord, and touch not the unclean *thing*; and I will
receive you.

1st Corinthians 3:16-17

16Know ye not that ye are the temple of God, and *that* the Spirit of
God dwelleth in you? 17If any man defile the temple of God, him

shall God destroy; for the temple of God is holy, which *temple* ye are.

We have to schedule personal time with God and ourselves just as we make it important to meet with potential clients. We need to love our bodies enough to take care of them.

Everyday, touch your body and say, " My body is the temple of the Holy Ghost and no sickness dwells within me. I rebuke and curse every seed of sickness in my body in the name of Jesus. I pull out every sickness from its root in the name of Jesus. According to Your word, Lord, life and death is in the power of my tongue; therefore, I will daily speak life over my body, family, businesses, church and my life in the name of Jesus."

- **Dieting** – Eat healthy and balanced meals. A healthy diet is one that helps us maintain or improve a general healthy condition. A healthy diet provides the body with essential nutrition. As we were told in primary school,
  a balanced diet contains the following food groups: protein, fats, fruits, vegetables, dairy and grains. Be deliberate to include those food groups in moderation in your meals. Speak to your doctor about healthy dieting as they can give you the necessary recommendation for the appropriate diet. This will help you think clearly, be healthier and live a longer life. If we want to reference the bible in Genesis, we know that plants were created for us to eat. I have had the opportunity to explore the JJ Smith Green smoothie (an author on healthy living) and it has made a difference in my health. If we go back to the basics and eat the things God created for us to eat, we will not experience all these medical issues that exist in today's society.

- **Resting** – We have been told since we were young that we need eight hours of sleep per night. As I get older, my doctor still encourages me to get eight hours of sleep per night because rest is good for the body in several ways. It's no different now; we need our rest so we are able to recharge our brain, help us to think much clearer and make better life decisions.

- **Doctor Visits** – The word of God teaches us to use wisdom in whatever we do. If you have access to medical coverage or even have the finances to go to the doctor, follow through on your routine medical checkups.

- **Exercise** – It is very important for us to exercise; it keeps our muscles flexible and strong. Exercise will improve our heart and blood vessels. In general, we will feel better about ourselves. When the Holy Spirit unctioned me to include physical fitness in this section, I asked God what was the relevance of physical fitness in regards to a successful business. The Holy Spirit responded, "Too many of my people are building businesses and are not able to reap the harvest because they neglect this area of their life. They are over worked, which is a sin. They do not have a balanced life. My desire for them is to have a prosperous life. Prosperous meaning be fulfilled in every area of their life."

    - Exercise one hour per day for at least four days per week or as your doctor recommends. It recharges the mind and helps the body to function properly as God intended. Exercise such as walking and/or any form of exercise that your doctor may recommend.

Spiritual

Strengthen Your Spiritual Relationship with God:

Developing a More Intimate Relationship with God Through Thanksgiving, Praise, Worship, Prayer, Fasting, and Meditating on Word of God

It's very important to build a relationship with God. He is our creator. He created us with a purpose. Therefore, it is important to know His plans and will for our life. If we are not walking in the will of God for our life, it will be a miserable one because we are not living on purpose. Think of God as our boss. Yes, we know we have free will. We have now decided to connect with our creator who will help us to live a fulfilling life. As we build a relationship with Him through thanksgiving, praising, worshiping, reading His word, praying and fasting, we will begin to hear Him clearer. God is always speaking to us; it's just that we are too busy with the cares of this world that it corrodes our frequency to hear Him. Do you wake-up in the morning telling your creator God good morning and thanking Him for sparing your life for another day? Do you tell your savior Jesus Christ good morning and do you ask the Holy Spirit what is your assignment for today? Have you asked the Holy Spirit to lead and direct you through the day and help you to complete your assignment for the day? If we consult with our creator on our day-to-day assignment, we will not find ourselves making wrong business decisions.

Take the time out every morning to pray before you start your day. Thank God, praise Him, worship Him, read His word and stop to listen and hear what He is saying to you. Investing in at least half an hour every morning to be in His presence can save you hours to correct an issue that God would have warned you about. Pray at midday and pray at night. The more time you spend with God, the more you will be tuned into His frequency (you will be able to hear Him) and the more you will know Him. Think of it this way: when you meet someone you are interested in, you begin to spend more time with them so you can get to know each other. You probably go to dinner, the movies and just walk and talk. You listen to each other. You speak on the phone. You then become acquainted to one another's voice. The more time you spend together, the more intimate you become and eventually, fall in love. It is basically the same concept. The more you read the word of God, the more He will reveal Himself to you and you will get to understand Him. As you praise Him, worship Him, talk to Him and listen to hear what His Spirit is saying to you, you will get direction on what decisions to make in life whether business or personal. Then as you mature and get in Him presence, you will know what He wants to do. You will know when He wants you to sing, to be still, to talk, to pray or what to do. You begin to understand what's on His mind and what's on His heart. You no longer limit the time you spend with Him because you are now in love and you don't want to leave His presence. He is more important to you now than anything or anyone in this world. Oh, what an awesome feeling. Two hours feel like five minutes. When you leave His presence, you are on a high that no drugs can take you to. You feel love. You release love. You feel joy. You release joy. You will now understand Psalms 34:8 KJV O taste and see that the LORD *is* good: blessed *is* the man *that* trusteth in him. His spirit within you that is magnified will allow you to make correct business and personal decisions.

Thanksgiving:

Our bible tells us in Psalm 100:4 [4] Enter into his gates with thanksgiving, *and* into his courts with praise: be thankful unto him, *and* bless his name.

We are to show thankfulness and gratitude for what God has done for us and what He is about to do for us. Thank Him for the air we breathe, the trees, plants and the basic things in life. This should be the first thing we do every time we get in the presence of God. Imagine that if you give someone something and they show you gratitude, then you will be encouraged to give them more. If they showed ungratefulness, then you would not feel appreciated and would be discouraged from giving them anything else. When we thank God, we are recognizing His goodness. This opens up the gate to enter into "His Courts." Thanksgiving is the utterance from our mouth. This act can loosen God's supernatural power in our life.

Praise:

Praise is recognizing God's greatness and marvelous work. This is an act of great sounds, shouts and dances that border on the ridiculous. People will look at you and thing you are crazy. Yes, crazy for God. This type of celebration breaks all barriers, piercing through hostile environments, and it gives us access to our creator through the Holy Spirit. This declaration of His powerful deeds will bring us into His presence. Thanksgiving and praise releases us from self.

Worship:

Worshiping God is an intimate, reverencing and respectful moment that produces life and is the birthing ground for miracles. This is the birthing place for ministries and businesses, and you can receive your healing. This is when we get to hear the voice of God. During thanksgiving and praise, we speak to God. Worshiping God is when He speaks to us. This is when we climax, we feel powerless, we can have angelic visitation, we can see more in the spiritual realm and nothing else matters but God. We recognize God's majestic power, work and glory. His glory that surrounds us is indescribable. There is joy, peace, love and tranquility in His presence.

During a praise and worship session at a conference that I attended, I was lost in the presence of God when I had a vision of a wide, deep puddle of mud and lots of people were in it. At the center of it was a large clean rock mounted above the mud. I was standing on the rock pulling people out of the mud. As I was pulling them out, they were being cleaned. I got discouraged for a second because it appeared as if most of the people were still in the mud. I closed my eyes and began to pray in my heavenly language and a supernatural strength overpowered me. I felt good in my spirit. I had more energy to pull more people faster out of the mud. A few minutes later, I opened my eyes and realized I had pulled out more than half the people out of the puddle of mud. I was encouraged and continued to pull the rest out.

For this season, I believe it's during worship, dreams and visions that God speaks to me the most. Remember, we are all unique so you will have to figure out when is it that you hear from God the most, and please don't box Him in regardingwhen to speak to you. He is God and He will speak whenever He chooses. Be a willing vessel to receive what He has to say to you.

Prayer:

Prayer is an essential part of walking with God. Luke 6:12 KJV And it came to pass in those days, that he went out into a mountain to pray, and continued all night in prayer to God. If Jesus who is so holy and sinless could pray all night, what about us? Prayer is a conversation from us to God. It's listening and talking to Him. Though we know there are different types of prayer, we will not be focusing on that now; but for the purpose of this assignment, I want to emphasize the importance of praying or talking to God and then being still to hear what the Holy Spirit has to say to you. Too often, we do a drive-by prayer, meaning we say quick prayer and rush off with our daily activities, not waiting to hear from God; and then we complain that God has not answered our prayers.

Praying in our heavenly language allows us to pray the perfect prayer (Romans 8:26), it build us up spiritually (1 Corinthians 14:4), drives depression and anxiety away (Isaiah 12:3), it keeps us in the love of God (Jude 20) and so much more benefits. Most times before I start to pray, I would ask the Holy Spirit how to pray. Sometimes I would ask God what's on His mind and what I should pray for. Most often, the Holy Spirit would impress upon me to pray for the country, our president and pastors. The Holy Spirit sometimes sends me to a shopping center to walk the parking lot and pray to bind up the spirit of death and release blessings over people. Sometimes the Holy Spirit will unction me to pray specific personalized prayer points for people walking by me. They all were clueless as to how much God loves them that He would interrupt my day to go and pray for them. I carry out my assignments without any of them knowing. That's how awesome God is, He is thinking of us when we are busy taking care of our day-to-day activities.

Avoid begging God every time you pray. Sometimes just praise Him or ask Him what you can do for Him today. Remember, when we take care of God's business, He will take care of us.

Fasting:

Fasting helps us to get a deeper revelation of who God is. Jesus said to Peter in Mark 9:29 [29]And he said unto them, This kind can come forth by nothing, but by prayer and fasting. Fasting kills the flesh so the spirit can manifest more. We have to understand that what we feed will thrive and what we starve will die. I was on a twenty-one day food fast when I realized that as I would pray for something, it would manifest almost immediately. One evening, I prayed and asked God to reveal to me my enemies. The same night, I dreamt I was at a place and I saw my clothes buried there. I took them up and in that same dream, I am reminded about a dream I had a few months before that one of my books that I had written had been on the ground with mud thrown on it. When I was awakened from the dream, I did not realize it was God answering my prayers that quickly. It was not until about midday during my prayer session that the Holy Spirit revealed it me. What I learned during that fasting session is that when we pray, minister or prophecy from the Glory Realm, manifestation of what we say is quick and almost immediate.

Meditating on the Word of God:

When we mediate on the word of God, we release the power of God in our life. Joshua 1:8 KJV This book of the law shall not depart out of thy mouth; but thou shalt meditate therein day and night, that thou mayest observe to do according to all that is written therein: for then thou shalt make thy way prosperous, and then thou shalt have good success. When we know the word of the Lord, we are not easily swayed to wrong doctrine. When we pray and apply the word of God, we get results because we are praying according to His principles.

How to Walk in the Supernatural Provision of God:

Some would say supernatural means relating to or being above or beyond what is natural, or unexplainable by natural law. I believe supernatural is an eternal realm that can only be accessed by faith. God is a supernatural being with supernatural ability. Our God is a supernatural God.

I believe in order for us to tap into the supernatural, we have to learn God's ways, likes and dislikes, and have a relationship with Him, a hunger for the supernatural and faith. Let's take a look at some of God's supernatural power.

Some Supernatural Ways of God in the Old Testament Days:

1. Genesis 1:3 And God said, Let there be light: and there was light. He spoke the words and natural things manifested
2. God destroyed the entire city of Sodom and Gomorrah with fire because of their wickedness. Genesis 19:23-25.
3. God blessed Abraham at age 100 and Sarah at age 90 with a son. Genesis 21:1-3.
4. God protected Moses as a baby from Pharaoh's plot to kill the first-born males of the Israelites, Exodus 2.
5. God spoke to Moses from a burning bush. Exodus 3.
6. In Egypt, God caused 10 plagues to hit the land when Pharaoh would not release His people (the children of Israel). Exodus 7.
7. God parted the Red Sea for the children of Israel to pass through safely and drowned Pharaoh's army. Exodus 13:17 and Exodus 14:29

8. In the wilderness, God caused manna to descend from heaven for the Israelites to eat. Exodus 16:1-24
9. God destroyed the wall of Jericho so the Israelites could take the city. Joshua 6
10. God caused an axe head to float on the water so it could be found. 2 Kings 6
11. God gave Samson the strength to kill a lion and tear down the columns of the Philistines. Judges 14 and 16
12. Young David killed the giant Goliath with a sling and a stone. 1 Samuel 17
13. The widow of Zarephath and her son were fed by God with the multiplication of oil and flour which sustained them for life. 1 Kings 17:8-15
14. God caused Balaam's donkey to speak. Numbers 22:28
15. God raised a man from the dead when Elisha's bones touched the man's body. 2 Kings 13:21
16. God kept Shadrach, Meshach and Abednego safe in the fire. Daniel 3
17. God protected Jonah in the whale belly and Daniel in the lion's den. Jonah 2:2

Some Supernatural Ways of God in the New Testament Days:

1. Jesus healed the centurion's servant by speaking the words from a distance. Matthew 8:5-13
2. Jesus multiplied five loaves and two fishes to feed a multitude of over 5000 that He was ministering to. Matthew 14:17-19
3. Jesus cursed a fig tree and it dried up. Matthew 21:18-21
4. Jesus healed Peter's mother-in-law. Luke 4:38-39
5. Jesus healed ten lepers. Luke 17:11-19
6. Jesus turned water into wine. John 2:3-11

7. Jesus raised Lazarus after he had been dead for four days. John 11:1-45

Some Supernatural Ways of God in My Life:

1. One winter afternoon of 2005 in New Jersey, I was driving with my three sons. We had just left church in Whippany. My sons were arguing and I was trying to meditate on the message I had just heard in service. My sons tried to get me involved in their argument but I told them to resolve the problem themselves. As their discussion got louder and more argumentative, I thought, "God, You said You would be a father to the fatherless; talk to them please. I just need some peace and quietness now, God." I was very frustrated to the point that I yelled, "Jesus!" When I did, our car spun around approximately three times on a busy, icy four-lane highway. We all saw death. I could hear the sound of breaks in every direction on the busy highway. Finally, our car stopped on the bank of the highway with the front pointing in a different direction than the flowing traffic. As I looked to check on my sons, they all had their hands bracing each other from being hurt. We all stared at each other and began to cry. Other vehicles stopped to check if we were ok and to try figure out what had just happened. No vehicle had crashed even though the highway was busy with heavy-flowing traffic. When we arrived home that evening, we hugged each other, cried and thanked God for sparing our lives. Needless to say from that day, my sons were changed more respectful of the way they spoke to each other in my presence. We would remind each other of that Sunday evening experience if one of us were to start an argument.

2. After I started into ministry full-time, I sold a BMW I had and sowed 50% of the proceeds to a ministry on behalf of my students' businesses. I purchased a cargo van for catering and other church activities. Approximately three years after purchasing it and fixing some issues with it, I was heading home one evening when it broke down on the street. I called a family member to come and get me. I packed everything of value I had in it and took it with me. I prayed over it, thanking God for it sustaining me as long as it did and I began to pray and ask God for debt-free transportation. Months later, the Holy Spirit told a lady name Vickie to bless me with a Dodge Durango. I did not pay a penny for it. Thank You, Jesus.
3. In 2011, I was getting ready for a business networking event when I decided to advertize the event on a Christian channel. I was to tape the promo first which would cost me $200. I had no money left in my account, but I knew the Holy Spirit wanted me to advertize the event. As I communicated with my contact person, Lady D, I explained to her that I did not have the money; she paused and told me we would figure it out. The money was to pay her camera guy. By faith, I proceeded to get dressed, praising and worshiping God all at once. When I was finished dressing, the Holy Spirit unctioned me to go to my ATM, insert my card and punch in $200. I paused and began question was that the voice of God or my imagination. Then I rebuked the spirit of doubt and proceeded as the Holy Spirit has indicated. I got to the ATM and thought to myself, what on earth am I doing? I arrived at the ATM and inserted my card to make the withdrawal for $200. I waited for a few seconds and the money started coming out the dispenser. I started screaming, "Hallelujah!!!" People were

looking at me as if I was crazy. I called Lady D and told her what had happened, and she joined me rejoicing over the phone.

4. One evening in 2013 as I was driving home, I stepped on my brakes could hear the metal hitting metal on my brake pad. I had no money to fix it and for few seconds, I felt sorry for myself and was at the point of crying. I heard a still voice say. "Practice what you teach." I stoped to think and then I remembered Malachi 3:8-13. I regained my confidence, held my head up and began to praise God. When I arrived home, I got out of my vehicle like a frustrated woman on a mission. I walked around it and began to pray and rebuke the devourer. Among other things, I said, "God, I give my tithes and offerings timely and correctly. I sow seeds for your Kingdom work. I am in covenant with You so right now, I dispatch Mechanical Angels to fix my vehicle." Yep, I had no clue that "Mechanical Angels" existed until that day. I cannot even tell you where the thought came from. I said, "Lord, You are mighty enough to heal the sick and raise the dead; surely, you can fix my vehicle." I prayed in my heavenly language for a few minutes. If you had seen me, you would have thought that I was losing my mind. To make a long testimony short, I concluded my prayer by thanking God for fixing my car. I released it into the hands of God. I went in my house and took a nap. Approximately two weeks later, my son and I were in the vehicle on our way to run an errand when my son asked, "Mom, how much did you pay to get the brakes fixed?" (He had previously heard the metal hitting metal when we applied brakes or just tried to stop). I screamed and yelled, "Hallelujah!!! Hallelujah!!! Hallelujah!!! Thank You, Jesus!!!" Now it did not make

sense how I had forgotten the brake problem and more importantly, I didn't realize it was supernaturally fixed. I told my son what I had done. My son who had lost his faith in God looked at me and said, "Why does God do stuff all the time for you?" I responded, "I try to live by God's law. I am in covenant with Him through tithing and offering. I trust Him and believe in Him. I have a relationship with Him and more importantly, I have faith in Him. My faith is not where I want it to be, but it is a work in progress."

5. One Saturday in 2013, I was at our church staff meeting when my pastor asked for us to donate money to fix the church ceiling. I had no money but the Holy Spirit said to pledge $100 and so I did. The Sunday morning when it was due, a few family members had blessed me with $80. Yes, I needed that money for gas and other things but I realized that was a part of the $100 seed. On my way to church that Sunday morning, I went to the bank to check my bank account which had no money in it but I was hoping God would repeat the miracle He had done for me before (money appearing in my bank account). At the bank, I parked my car. I did not go through the drive-through. As I approached the bank door to open it, I saw $20 on the floor. I cried. I praised God. Yes, I did look around to see if anyone was there to claim it and there was no one in sight, so I picked it up and got in my car and gave the $100 to help fix the ceiling at my church.
6. In 2014, I presented to God three conferences that I wanted to attend. One to be held in Atlanta with Bishop TD Jakes, another in Tampa with Dr. Rodney Howard Brown and the third in Miami with Apostle Guillermo Maldonado. I did not have the first penny to purchase the event tickets or for flights and transportation. All the money God blessed me

with would go back into the ministry work after tithes, offering, gas and personal necessities. Supernaturally, the Holy Spirit told a young lady named Fetu to bless me with the ticket, transportation and hotel accommodation for the Atlanta conference. My sons sponsored my Miami and Tampa trips. On my way back from the Miami conference, which was about the supernatural, I had sown all the food money I had and was left with only gas money to the penny. I could not even afford a McDonald's 99-cent sandwich. I was happy, in fact very happy, because my spirit was filled with the teaching and praise and worship service I had received from Apostle Maldonado and his team. As I started on my 3½ to 4 hour drive back to Orlando, I began to praise and worship God. I listened to some inspirational messages. Approximately 45 minutes away from home, I said to God, "Daddy, I could sure eat some food now." The Holy Spirit said, "Use your debit card; money is in your account." I pulled up at an ATM, checked my account balance and surely there was money in it. I got excited, stopped into a store and picked up some stuff. I got to the cash register and nervousness kicked in with the devil telling me that I'm going to be embarrassed. The lady rang up my stuff I handed her my card nervous as ever. She swiped it and I saw it was approved. I said, "Thank You, Jesus," with relief. I went home logged on to my bank account and could not trace where the money came from.

7. In 2014, I was at a prophetic conference when God told a prophet to tell me to sow all the money I had in my bank account and pocket book. I didn't even hesitate. I sowed everything I had as the prophet had instructed. Upon leaving the church, I realized when I got in my car that my

gas tank was on empty and I had no money left to buy gas. I prayed by faith and drove home 1½ hours on an empty tank.

All the above are some examples of the supernatural power of God. You, too, can experience it as you apply faith and continue to build an intimate relationship with God, the Holy Spirit and Jesus. Study the word of God. Have a hunger for the supernatural things of God and be led by the Holy Spirit. We serve a supernatural God. God wants to do supernatural things in our lives, ministries, careers and businesses. We are in a supernatural season. Let us position ourselves for the manifestation of the supernatural work of God.

How to Hear the Voice of God:

1. Build a relationship with God through:
    a. Prayer
    b. Praise and worship
    c. Fasting
    d. Reading the word of God
    e. Meditating upon the word of God
    f. Communing with the Holy Spirit

Please refer back to the spiritual section which will elaborate more on prayer, praise, worship, fasting and meditating on the word of God.

2. Have faith in God and trust Him. When God speaks, sometimes it doesn't make sense; just do it and later you will understand why later.
    a. Hebrews 11:1 Now faith is the substance of things hoped for, the evidence of things not seen
    b. Hebrews 11:6 But without faith it is impossible to please him: for he that cometh to God must believe

that he is, and that he is a rewarder of them that diligently seek him

3. Be obedient to God
    a. What is the Holy Spirit telling you to do?
        i. Go to the hospital and pray?
        ii. Pray for Jerusalem?
        iii. Is He waking you up at night to pray?
4. Have a hunger for the supernatural things of God
    a. What we crave will eventually manifest in our life. Now think of it: if you desire to have ice cream, that craving won't go away until you have satisfied it. You will drive a mile until you find the right flavor and brand ice cream you are looking for. Similarly for the things of God, when I have a hunger for a specific gifting from God, I begin to pray, study and fast for God to let such gifting manifest in my life. We know that God gives us the desires of our heart. I won't give up until my spirit is at ease about the situation and I begin to see manifestation of the gifting in my life.

Summary:

- **Thanksgiving** recognizes God's goodness. We speak to God. We choose to worship Him. It's utterance from our mouth. This opens up the gate to His courts. Psalm 100:4 KJV [4]Enter into his gates with thanksgiving, *and* into his courts with praise: be thankful unto him, *and* bless his name.

- **Praising** is exalting God with powerful sounds, shouts and dance that make you look outrageous as we speak to God. This is our decision which brings us into His courts. When we celebrate God's greatness and goodness, it breaks barriers and releases us from self.

- **Worship** is an intimate moment with God for birthing and healing; it is an utterance from our heart. God speaks to us. It's God decision to respond as we touch His heart.
- **Thanksgiving:** God hears our voice.
- **Praise:** God hears our voice.
- **Worship:** We get to hear God's voice.
- **Prayer** is a verbal communication with God. After you have prayed, be still to hear what He has to say.
- **Fasting** suppresses the flesh so spirit manifests more. It clears the airwaves to hear what God is saying to us.
- **Thanksgiving and praise** release us from ourselves. It's not about us, it about magnifying our creator God.
- **Supernatural:** Be in an expecting mood as you praise and worship God. If we expect nothing, then we will get nothing. According to Hebrews 11:1 [1]Now faith is the substance of things hoped for, the evidence of things not seen.

<u>Some Things That We Can Do to Magnify the Presence of God in Our Life:</u>

- Close our eyes as we praise and worship God, as this will block us from seeing things that will take our focus away from His presence.

- If you are in a church setting, be in one accord with your worship leader. You can cause a curse on yourself for causing a disruption of the flow of the Holy Spirit. Romans 15:6 and Acts 2:1-3 remind us that God is a God of order; and as we unify together in His presence, we will begin to see miracles, signs and wonders.

- Have a visual of God and His presence.

- Ask the Holy Spirit to lead you. Let the Holy Spirit lead you. What God tells you to do sometimes doesn't make sense. ***Just be obedient; just do it!!!*** You will see His mighty hand at work. You will see miracles, signs and wonders. I was in service once and during deep worship, the Holy Spirit told me to go and lay at the altar. I began to reason with the Holy Spirit and kneel at my seat because I was too shy to do so. As I knelt at my seat, I felt like the presence of God in the atmosphere shifted. I began to repent. I went to the altar as the Holy Spirit had urged me to do. A few minutes later, the prophet who was ministering began to pray for me, prophecy to me and give an impartation to me. Now I believed I would have missed out on that opportunity of God ministering to me had I not obeyed the Holy Spirit.

- Benefits of praising and worshiping God are as follows: You don't have to wait for your pastor or leaders to lay hands on you to receive your healing. You can praise and worship God and get your healing and deliverance during your individual or corporate worshiping. I remember going to a Pastor Benny Hinn service and during worship, people in wheelchairs were being healed without anyone touching them or praying for them. God's glory manifests where praise is high and worship is deep. We can receive our healing and deliverance in such atmosphere. Most of the time as I praise and worship God in His presence, that's when He would give me new chapters for my book and what message to teach His people.

- When worship is deep, healing, deliverance, creative miracles, impartation and birthing of new ideas can take place.

As you create an atmosphere for God to dwell in, know that His will is being done in your life, because now the frequency is clear to hear God voice. It's not that He wasn't talking to us before but because we were so busy with the cares of life, our frequency was eroded and we couldn't hear Him.

When all is said and done, there is a key component that plays a major role in the manifestation of God's will for our life, and that is faith. In Hebrews 11:1 KJV [1]Now faith is the substance of things hoped for, the evidence of things not seen. Also, we have seen in Hebrews 11:32-33 how David, Samson and many other prophets were able to subdue kingdoms through faith. So if you have faith, believing that your business will be successful, then it will be. If you have faith that you will receive your healing, then you will. Read and meditate on Hebrews 11. Pray and ask the Holy Spirit to help you understand the importance of faith.

Applying Faith to God's Will for Your Life is Crucial

When God gives you an assignment or puts in your heart to do something, it will always look impossible through your eyes. It might be lack of finances or resources, health issues or a lack of confidence in our own capability. This section will help you understand the importance of having faith to do the impossible things God is telling you to do. Hebrews 11:6 [6]But without faith *it is* impossible to please *him*: for he that cometh to God must believe that he is, and *that* he is a rewarder of them that diligently seek him. If you do what you can, then God will do the rest.

What is Faith?

- Faith is divine ability given to man to go beyond the natural realm
- Faith enables us to see into the supernatural
- Faith is our response to the mind of God
- Faith activates the promises of God from the supernatural to the natural realm

Hebrews 11:1 KJV Now faith is the substance of things hoped for, the evidence of things not seen.

How Important is Faith to God?

Hebrews 11:6 KJV But without faith it is impossible to please him: for he that cometh to God must believe that he is, and that he is a rewarder of them that diligently seek him.

Faith looks at the impossible and sees possibilities: John 11:40 [40] Jesus saith unto her, Said I not unto thee, that, if thou wouldest believe, thou shouldest see the glory of God? Proverbs 3:5 Trust in the Lord with all thine heart and lean not to thine own understanding

We walk by faith and not by sight: 2 Corinthians 5:7 [7] For we walk by faith, not by sight. To live in victory we have to have faith. Trials will come our way to force us to see the invisible promises of God and to distract us from God's promises. It is for us to trust God and use our faith to see His promises manifest in our life. Reminder we cannot experience where our mind have not seen. Our blessings are dependent on our ability to see it in the now.

Pray the word of God over our situation: Romans 10:17 [17] So then faith cometh by hearing, and hearing by the word of God. Study the word of God. Pray the word of God. For example if you are praying for healing, "Lord your word says in Isaiah 53:5 (KJV) But he *was* wounded for our transgressions, *he was* bruised for our iniquities: the chastisement of our peace *was* upon him; and with his stripes we are healed. Therefore, Lord by Your stripes I receive your healing power manifesting in my body right now in Jesus' name, Amen!" When we pray the word of God, He will respond; so whatever your situations/challenges in life might be, apply the word of God to it as you pray and believe for its manifestation in your life.

When God speaks to us we have to trust Him consistently: When we doubt Him, we allow access to the devil. We have to trust God always and know that His timing is not ours. He will manifest His will for our life as He chooses. Romans 4:20-21 [20] He staggered not at the promise of God through unbelief; but was strong in faith, giving glory to God; [21] And being fully persuaded that, what he had promised, he was able also to perform.

Whatever we believe will manifest in our life: Matthew 9:29 [29] Then touched he their eyes, saying, According to your faith be it unto you. Your faith activates the unseen promises of God. Faith only works if you work it. Take a leap of faith to do what the Holy Spirit is telling you to do. If you start it, God will finish it. Do what you can and God will do the rest. Each and every one of us has been given a measure of faith and what we do with it is solely up to us. Romans 12:3 [3] For I say, through the grace given unto me, to every man that is among you, not to think of himself more highly than he ought to think; but to think soberly, according as God hath dealt to every man the measure of faith.

Romans 1:17-18 [17] For therein is the righteousness of God revealed from faith to faith: as it is written, The just shall live by faith. [18] For the wrath of God is revealed from heaven against all ungodliness and unrighteousness of men, who hold the truth in unrighteousness. Max out the level of faith you are given and God will increase your faith. Mark 9:23 [23] Jesus said unto him, If thou canst believe, all things are possible to him that believeth. Faith is the channel that makes God's possibility available to you.

You feed your faith and starve your doubt by studying and meditating upon the word of God that speaks about faith. Your trust in God will grow. When He speaks to your spirit to do the impossible in your career, business or ministry, it will be much easier because you understand faith.

When you have done all you can, rest in the presence of God; praise and worship Him, knowing that He will do for you what you can't do for yourself. There is the silent moment to test your faith. When you cannot hear from God, you have to be careful what you say because you can abort your blessing if your mummer, complain and speak negatively over your situation. Life and death is in the power of your tongue. Sometimes we believe that God is not listening to us and we begin to have doubt which will allow access to the devil. Trust God and be still; wait for Him to manifest His promises on His time frame. Our God is not a God that lies.

What is it God has told you to do but because of a lack of faith, you are still stuck?

- Get in the presence of God (praise, worship, pray, meditate and read His word).
- See your future according to what God is speaking to you about. Renew your mind.
- Do what God is telling you to do. Do what you can and God will do the rest.
- Remember that faith is the substance of things hoped for and evidence of things not seen.
- It is by activating your faith you will receive your breakthrough and your blessings from God.
- It is by activating your faith you will receive your healing.
- It is by activating your faith you will receive miracles, signs and wonders in your life.
- It is by activating your faith you can please God (Hebrew 11:6).
- It is by activating your faith you step out to do the impossible things that God is stirring your spirit to do.
- It is by faith we receive the benefits Jesus provided on the cross: salvation, health, deliverance, prosperity, peace and all emotional and spiritual provision.
- Your faith must be accompanied by action. Faith without works is dead.

Faith Declarations

Remember, what you speak over your life will manifest in your life. Say aloud:

- I receive the gift of faith by faith
- My faith will not fail
- I walk by faith and not by sight
- By faith, I receive the promises of God in my life
- My faith and hope are in God
- I have the faith anointing
- I have extraordinary faith and it's manifesting in and through me

Tithes and Offering

I want to share with you seven blessings you receive if you bring your tithes and offerings to the storehouse of God. You will not be financially successful in life if you don't tithe, give offerings and sow seeds. Pray and fast all you can, financial blessings will not manifest in your life if Tithing and Offering foundation is not established. When you give your tithes and offerings, you enter into a covenant with God and the following seven blessings will manifest in your life.

Malachi 3-8 8 Will a man rob God? Yet ye have robbed me. But ye
say, Wherein have we robbed thee? In tithes and offerings. 9 Ye *are*
cursed with a curse: for ye have robbed me, *even* this whole nation.
10 Bring ye all the tithes into the storehouse, that there may be meat
in mine house, and prove me now herewith, saith the LORD of
hosts, if I will not open you the windows of heaven, and pour you
out a blessing, that *there shall* not *be room* enough *to receive it.*
11 And I will rebuke the devourer for your sakes, and he shall not
destroy the fruits of your ground; neither shall your vine cast her

fruit before the time in the field, saith the LORD of hosts. [12]And all nations shall call you blessed: for ye shall be a delightsome land, saith the LORD of hosts.

1. ***Open Heavens:*** When the heavens are open, there are no hindrances in our communication to God. We have clear frequency. This can birth revival in our homes, churches, jobs, ministries and businesses. What's dead in our lives will come alive according to God's will.

2. ***Pour out Blessings*:** Can you imagine God pouring out His blessings on us? Imagine living a prosperous and abundant life. A life with no sickness and no financial issues. In life, we know problems will come but they will not consume us. The grace, favor and mercy of God will sustain us.

3. ***Rebuke the Devourer for My Sake:*** To rebuke means to cripple or paralyze any unexpected spending the devil might try to attack you with. Have you ever noticed that the minute you receive extra money or a bonus check, your car begins to have problems or some unexpected issues come up that you have to use that money to compensate for?

4. ***Harvest is Protected*:** You will not unexpectedly or wastefully spend money. Your money will multiply.

5. ***Fruitfulness:*** I will be prosperous in whatever I do and my children are protected. John 15:5 I am the vine, ye are the branches.

6. ***International Recognition:*** People of all cultures will know of you and your offspring by way of positive deeds.

7. ***Favor:*** You will be highly desired. You will have favor from God and man.

Seed

Although tithes and offerings is the foundation of financial success, we must understand that sowing seeds is relevant to the dimension of financial success we achieve in life. Genesis 8:22 KJV While the earth remaineth, seedtime and harvest, and cold and heat, and summer and winter, and day and night shall not cease. It's important to sow financial seeds if you desire financial harvests/blessings. Remember the phrase, "The seed you sow, you shall reap"? It simply means that if you plant an apple seed, you will reap an apple tree. Therefore, sow financial seed to reap financial blessings; just be led by the Holy Spirit so that you will sow it in "good (fertile) grounds."

God is not moved by our needs. He is moved by our purpose. If you pray for financial blessings, its ultimate purpose is to be a blessing to someone. For example, if someone who prays for financial blessing so they could buy food to cook for the hungy in the community and someone who prays for financial blessing to buy the twentieth pair of shoes because they are a shoe lover, then the purpose-driven prayer will manifest quicker. What you give is what God will multiply.

Eight Keys to a Prosperous Life

1. Have a relationship with God and put God first in everything you do.

2. Know who you are and what you were created to do.
    - Who are you?
    - What's your identity?
    - What makes you, you?
    - What is the meaning of your name?

- Know the meaning of your date of birth and know it is also relevant to who you are and who were created to be. My name is Janet, which means a gift from God. During the early years of my parents' marriage, my mom had a miscarriage of the first child she was pregnant with. Both she and my dad fasted and pray to God for a child. They promised God that they would dedicate that child back to Him for Kingdom work. Several years later, I was born. My parents named me Janet not knowing what the meaning of my name was. I came to them as a gift from God. They named me Janet not knowing the symbolism of my name, but God did.

3. Have faith in God as He processes (trains) you to be who He has created you to be. Surrender to the process; do not speak negatively or curse your process.

4. How are you going to complete your destiny?

    - What steps are you taking to develop yourself in accordance with your purpose?
    - What's your personal vision?
    - What's your personal mission statement? My mission statement is: *To be a generational changer and a mighty woman of God with the purpose of living God's will for my life while teaching and coaching others to live God's will for their life.*

5. Have a mentor and some prayer partners. They should be people who believe and support your dreams and visions.

6. Be an expert in your area of gifting. 2 Timothy 2:15 Study to shew thyself approved unto God, a workman that needeth not to be ashamed, rightly dividing the word of truth. Knowledge is power. Study and learn your areas of gifting. Attend conferences and workshops, and read and listen to materials relating to your area of gifting. It's very important to let the Holy Spirit be your guide as to what materials you read and who you listen to for guidance and development. You should see fruits in them that you desire in your life. They should know how to motivate you.

7. You must sow seeds to reap a harvest. Sow seeds of labor and finances not just to any ministry, but let the Holy Spirit lead you where to sow your talent and finances.

8. As God blesses you, be a blessing to someone else. Be a mentor to someone else. We are blessed to be a blessing to others.

Call to Action Excercise

- Start your day and end your day with God. Schedule God in your day until it becomes a habit. He is first. If you spend your first half an hour or even one hour to praise, worship and meditate on the word of God, I guarantee you that you will have better days. He will warn you of traps that the devil set for you. God will protect you from the enemy and give you wisdom and knowledge on how to deal with obstacles you will encounter, or He will sometimes give you the strategy of how to remove it. God will give you good success. God is always speaking to us, but we are too busy with day-to-day activities; that's why we are not able to hear Him. We need to invest in quiet time with Him.

- Are you the smartest one in your inner circle? If so, this means everyone is pulling from your knowledge and you have no one you can learn from. It's time to change friends or get some new friends.

- Connect with positive business-minded people. Start to visit business networking events in your area. Join a Christian business group and or groups relating to your area of interest.

- Communicate your dreams of owning your own business or starting a ministry with your significant other. Reminder, they are not the one God give the vision to; therefore, don't be disappointed if they don't share the same enthusiasm as you do towards this new assignment. They cannot see it the way you do; they cannot feel the same passion you do. It's your assignment; therefore, you will feel more joy and excitement towards this new assignment. God allows you to see it because that's your assignment. Use or ask for their help in areas they are good at. For example, if your teenage child knows how to work the Internet, let them help you setup your Facebook business page. Before you know it, they are just as excited as you are. You are soliciting their passion without them knowing. Your approach and attitude will determine the response and corporation you receive from them. Use wisdom to solicit their help without them knowing what you are doing. Don't force them; you will kill the fun and potential positive support.

- Begin to pray and ask the Holy Spirit to help you select a mentor and prayer partners. These should be people you can confide in who have your best interest at heart.

Chapter Assignment

- Exercise at least 15 minutes per day. Consult your physician. Start with light exercise such as walking.
- Spend quality time with God each day praying and reading His word. Start and end your day with Him. Increase your time with Him weekly. Remember, God is the only one knows the beginning to the end of this assignment, so you want to have a close relationship with Him so He will give you step by step direction. This will save you years of costly mistakes.
- Start to disconnect from all your negative associations, people who speak negatively of your dreams. If it's your spouse, pray and ask God to touch their heart and help them to realize this assignment you are created for. Do not divorce them for this. Trust God, He will touch the heart of your spouse and help him/her to be supportive of God's will for your life.
- Start to develop positive associations by joining groups of like minds; for example, join your local chamber of commerce.
- Fast at least one day this week. Fasting does not have to be from food. It could be from your phone, Internet, Facebook or so forth (something that you enjoy doing).
    - Pray and ask ***God to close all doors that need to be closed and open doors that need to be opened in your life***. **Warning:** You must be ready for changes before you pray this prayer. You must be ready to get on the path God has created you for. There will

be people and things leaving your life. It will hurt in the beginning, but it will all be worth it. When I prayed this prayer, I transitioned from a 15-year job to full-time ministry with not even making 10% of what I usually make, and a man I was engaged to broke up with me within hours of this prayer. But I can truly say it was all worth it. I am a much happier person now and I am living God's will for my life. The prayer is: **"Dear Lord Jesus, close all doors in my life that need to be closed and open doors that need to be opened in Jesus' name, Amen!!!"**

  - Ask God's guidance and direction for your new business or ministry.
  - Pray and ask God to develop your hearing so you can hear His voice clearly. Pray and bind every demonic spirit that would try to speak to you in the name of Jesus.
  - Start sowing seed with your talent. Sign up to volunteer in a ministry at your church, local hospital or somewhere in your community that has relevance to your calling.

- Read Psalm 1 and Psalm 91 daily. Psalm 1 is a scripture for prosperity in business or ministry and Psalm 91 is a prayer of protection for yourself and your family. As you build your ministry, you have to learn how to build and fight at the same time and not be overwhelmed with either of the two. Having a balance is crucial so if you start now as you build your business and challenges come across your path, you will know which scripture to apply to your situation. Remember, the devil is not going to sit down and watch you try to live God's will for your life without a fight. Yes, I believe with you that you will be victorious but you have to work at it. If the devil tempted Jesus, why would he not try to tempt us? Study the word of God so you can and will recognize Him when He speaks to you.

- Pray for forgiveness of the sins for yourself, children and spouse. Read Psalm 51 daily so there will be no blockage in your life to hinder God's blessings from flowing.
- Pray and ask the Holy Spirit to activate the supernatural manifestations in your life.
- Pray for your faith to be increased as well as your relationship with the Holy Spirit.

Chapter Notes

Chapter To-Do List

Chapter Two

Personal Development

Please use this week to complete the form below honestly. No one will see the result unless you decide to share it. This graph will give you an idea about how you spent your time. You can then make the necessary adjustment with what you do with your time. In a later chapter, I will ask you again to complete this same diagram. The second time you complete this exercise you should have a different outcome because you have learned the importance of spending more time with God and focusing on things that will help you grow and develop yourself as a business owner or minister of what God has called you to do.

My Time Spent Per 24 Hours Exercise

Reminder: "Junk in, Junk out" Whatever you spent your time doing will manifest in your life.

	TV/ Internet	Family/ Work	Self / Exercise	Praying/ Meditating on God Word	Sleep	
Monday	2 hours/3 hours	1 hours /11 hours	30 minutes/ 20 minutes	10 minutes	6 hours	24 Hours
Tuesday						24 Hours
Wednesday						24 Hours
Thursday						24 Hours
Friday						24 Hours
Saturday						24 Hours
Sunday						24 Hours

Note: The phrase "Junk in Junk Out" means that whatever you listen to will manifest in your life; so if you want good success in your life, listen to positive things pertaining to your destiny. If you listen to negative news, it will feed on your doubt and insecurity. Allow your eardrum to have access to positive things that will help to build you up. Be a good steward to your eardrum, mind and spirit.

Unforgiveness

When God gave me this assignment of teaching people "How to Start a Business/Ministry," I asked Him what unforgiveness had to do with business. He responded, "I cannot bless My people fully because there are blockages in their life." When we live in unforgiveness, the blessings of God cannot flow freely in our life. This got me curious so I began to study unforgiveness and its fruit, and what I found out was shocking to me.

- Unforgiveness is like drinking poison and waiting for the other person to die. It means: Reluctant to forgive or admit one is wrong; Hang onto a negative feeling about someone who you feel has done something wrong to you; A feeling of resentment or ill will over some grievance, or to harbor resentment; Carrying around a feeling of resentment over some grievance; A feeling of deep and bitter anger; A long-standing resentment that carries with it a deep-seated feeling of spite, bitterness and hostility.
- What happens when you do **NOT** forgive someone?
    - High blood pressure
    - Stressed

- Hostile
- Anger management problem
- Heart rate problem
- High risk of alcohol or substance abuse
- Depression symptoms
- Anxiety symptoms
- Chronic pain
- Less or no friends
- No positive or healthy human relationships
- No religious or spiritual well-being
- Poor psychological well-being (make poor decisions)

What Does Our Bible Say About Unforgivess?

Leviticus 19:18 KJV Thou shalt not avenge, nor bear any grudge against the children of thy people, but thou shalt love thy neighbour as thyself: I *am* the LORD.

Matthew 18:23-35: Tells us it is our responsibility to forgive others

Matthew 6 Reminds us that unforgiveness prevents God from forgiving our sins because we do not forgive others.

Mark 11:24-25, Matthew 7:7 and Matthew 12 Shows us that unforgiveness can block God from answering our prayers

God can give us the strength to do it and He is very willing to help us if we will come to Him, ask and be willing to change (Isaiah 40:29-31, 41:10; Philippians 4:13; Matthew 11:28-30).

Take a few minutes of uninterrupted time to do the following exercise:

- Think about everyone you have a grudge with and write their name on a piece of paper.
- Give yourself permission to forgive them.
- Forgive everyone you have held a grudge with.
- Pray and ask God to forgive you for holding onto unforgiveness in your heart.
- As you pray to God, ask Him for the courage and grace to forgive anyone now or in the future who has done or will do you wrong.
- Pray and ask God to reveal any unforgiveness in your heart.
- Speak to the individual/individuals and ask for forgiveness. Let them know that you have forgiven them.
- Reminder: It's your responsibility to forgive them but it's not your responsibility for them to forgive you; so if they choose not to forgive you, it is well. You have done your part by forging them.
- Then pray and thank God that you are able to forgive and move on towards His plans for your

life. Now do everything you can to maintain a forgiving heart. Read Psalm 51 every night (this is a scripture of daily forgiveness). Remember, the bible tells us that offenses WILL come. People close to us will offend us, sometimes deliberately and sometimes not. It's for us to know how to deal with it when it comes. Do not harbor unforgiveness in your heart.

Please schedule uninterrupted time with yourself to complete this exercise. Take a few minutes to think about everyone that you have a grudge or unforgiveness with. Write their name(s) on a piece of paper. Give yourself permission to forgive them. As you rip the paper into small pieces, pray and thank God for giving you the courage to forgive each person. Ask God to give you the strength, courage and grace as you reach out to each person for forgiveness. Speak to the individuals and ask them for forgiveness. Release them or the situation and then pray and thank God that you are able to forgive and move towards His plan for your life. Wow! What a liberating feeling. Do not rob yourself of God's ultimate blessings for your life.

Loving you and forgiving yourself daily will help keep you on track for a healthier you. Speak positively over your life and those you come in contact with will help through this process.

Be deliberate to say:

- Three positive things each day for the next thirty days to family members in your household
- Two positive things each day for the next thirty days to coworkers you see everyday

- Five positive things each day for the next thirty days to yourself as you look in the mirror
- One positive thing each day for the next thirty days to two different strangers

Do not say anything negative to anyone for the next thirty days. For every negative thing you say, give a $1 yo a charitable organization in your community.

Pray with thanksgiving for the next thirty days. Do not ask God for anything for the next seven days. Just thank Him and ask what you can do for Him. Be still and listen with your ears and spirit when you are finished praying so you can hear what the Holy Spirit is responding to you.

Daily Declaration Scriptures

Matthew 7:7-8

7 Ask, and it shall be given you; seek, and ye shall find; knock, and
it shall be opened unto you: 8 For every one that asketh receiveth;
and he that seeketh findeth; and to him that knocketh it shall be
opened.

Proverbs 11:27

27 He that diligently seeketh good procureth favour: but he that seeketh mischief, it shall come unto him.

Matthew 17:20

20 And Jesus said unto them, Because of your unbelief: for verily I say unto you, If ye have faith as a grain of mustard seed, ye shall say unto this mountain, Remove hence to yonder place; and it shall remove; and nothing shall be impossible unto you.

Luke 6:38

38Give, and it shall be given unto you; good measure, pressed down, and shaken together, and running over, shall men give into your bosom. For with the same measure that ye mete withal it shall be measured to you again.

Luke 1:28

28And the angel came in unto her, and said, Hail, thou that art highly favoured, the Lord is with thee: blessed art thou among women.

Deuteronomy 8:18

18But thou shalt remember the LORD thy God: for it is he that giveth thee power to get wealth, that he may establish his covenant which he sware unto thy fathers, as it is this day.

Psalm 112:3

3Wealth and riches shall be in his house: and his righteousness endureth for ever.

2 Corinthians 9:8

8And God is able to make all grace abound toward you; that ye, always having all sufficiency in all things, may abound to every good work:

1 Peter 5:7

7Casting all your care upon him; for he careth for you.

Psalm 1:3

3And he shall be like a tree planted by the rivers of water, that bringeth forth his fruit in his season; his leaf also shall not wither; and whatsoever he doeth shall prosper.

Proverbs 10:22

22The blessing of the LORD, it maketh rich, and he addeth no sorrow with it.

Deuteronomy 28:8

8The LORD shall command the blessing upon thee in thy storehouses, and in all that thou settest thine hand unto; and he shall bless thee in the land which the LORD thy God giveth thee.

Psalm 37:4

4Delight thyself also in the LORD: and he shall give thee the desires of thine heart.

Malachi 3:10-11

10Bring ye all the tithes into the storehouse, that there may be meat
in mine house, and prove me now herewith, saith the LORD of
hosts, if I will not open you the windows of heaven, and pour you
out a blessing, that there shall not be room enough to receive it.
11And I will rebuke the devourer for your sakes, and he shall not
destroy the fruits of your ground; neither shall your vine cast her
fruit before the time in the field, saith the LORD of hosts.

Isaiah 54:17

17No weapon that is formed against thee shall prosper; and every tongue that shall rise against thee in judgment thou shalt condemn.

This is the heritage of the servants of the LORD, and their righteousness is of me, saith the LORD.

3 John 1:2

2Beloved, I wish above all things that thou mayest prosper and be in health, even as thy soul prospereth.

Deuteronomy 28:1

1And it shall come to pass, if thou shalt hearken diligently unto the voice of the LORD thy God, to observe and to do all his commandments which I command thee this day, that the LORD thy God will set thee on high above all nations of the earth

Deuteronomy 28:12

12The LORD shall open unto thee his good treasure, the heaven to give the rain unto thy land in his season, and to bless all the work of thine hand: and thou shalt lend unto many nations, and thou shalt not borrow.

God Can Use Us if We Submit to Him

Be positive and know that if God can use these people with all their flaws, what about you?

- Esther – Adopted – She became a Persian Queen and helped the Jews to be delivered
- Job – Bankrupt – God restored him double for his troubles
- Jeremiah – Insecure – He was a mighty prophet of God
- Rahab – Prostitute – Yet she was in Jesus' genealogy
- Isaiah – Day Dreamer – He was a Prophet of God

- Leah – Unattractive – She gave birth to six tribes of Israel
- Gideon – Afraid and Intimidated – He had victory over the Medians
- Jonah – Prejudiced – God used him to warn the people of Nineveh
- Peter – Coward – He was sent to the Gentiles
- David – Murderer – God called him a man after His own heart
- Abraham – Liar – God called him friend
- Paul – Hit-Man – Wrote two-thirds of the New Testament
- Jacob – Manipulator – Named Israel and called a prince
- Joseph – Abuse and Rejected – He was promoted from prison to palace
- Moses – Stuttering – Lead the children of Israel out of bondage
- Samson – Womanizer – Judge of Israel

There is nothing God will not forgive you of except blasphemy against the Holy Ghost. Remember, we have free will. God is a gentleman; He will not force Himself on us. So you have to be at the place of your life where you are willing and ready for change and want Him in your life.

Chapter Assignment

- Exercise at least 20 minutes each day for five days per week.
- Spend quality time with God each day, thanking Him for this new venture.
- Begin to praise God and thank Him for answering your prayers.
- Thank God for choosing you for this new venture.
- Separate yourself from all negative people.
- Continue to develop new and positive relationships.
- Meet with your immediate family members to communicate your new business venture and solicit their help (pray before and after your meetings). Schedule a meeting time and place that is suitable for everyone involved.
- Fast at least one day this week.
- Continue sowing seeds of your talents and offerings.
- Give your tithes (10% of all income you receive).
- Read Psalm 1 and Psalm 91 daily.

Chapter Notes

Chapter To-Do List

Chapter Three

Staying Faithful to God Through All Stages of Life

For the purpose of this exercise, we are going to discuss "Seasons of Our Life" as three stages of life.

Season One: Instantaneous Blessings

Season one is when God supplies all your needs immediately. Everything you pray for, He grants it to you in a short period of time. Every part of your personal life is going great. Below are some of the events that usually happen in season one:

- Your children are doing great in school.
- There is harmony in your home; husband, wife, children and pets are happy.
- You have a successful career. Every year, your job review is awesome. You and your coworkers are good friends. You have social gatherings together and everyone is happy and in unity. You look forward to going to work functions together and you really enjoy each other's company. You have a pleasant work environment. You are earning the highest pay rate for your pay grade. Life is just fabulous.
- You have the latest module car. You have a boat that you use for weekend getaways.
- Your savings account is well maintained and your stock investment is thriving.
- You are able to take two family vacations of your choice annually.

Season One Action: What Do You Do?

- Thank, praise and worship God.
- Pray and read the word of God as a family unit. My mother usually says, "A family that prays together, stays together."
- Share the wealth with whosoever you can bless. Join a community service agency and volunteer as a family unit.
- Be deliberate to give to the poor and needy. Drive to areas of your community where they are people less fortunate than you and bless them with food and clothing, and minister to them the word of God.
- Give your tithes and offering. Sow your talent and money to help further the Kingdom of God.

Season Two: Am I Suffering or Am I Reaping?

When you are in your second season, what you usually depend on God to do immediately will stop or take forever to manifest.

- Children begin to have problems in school. They are suspended from sports club at school. Their grades are declining.
- You begin to have unexpected expenses. You are not able to save money; in fact, your savings account is decreasing dramatically. You are losing money on investments.
- You now only have one income. Your spouse with the strongest financial backing has lost his/her job and the other spouse is experiencing problems at work and is on the verge of losing his/her job also.

- Because of the financial stress in the home, there is no harmony in your home. Husband and wife are arguing. Children and pets are being neglected. Everyone is looking out for themselves.

- People who you thought were your friends turned against you. They are now your enemies. They gossip about your challenges and have separated themselves from you and your family. You are now the "talk of the town." You realize all your pals have disappeared and they do not respond to your calls or e-mails. You have to sell your boat because you need the money for your house mortgage. You are not able to take family vacations anymore.

- **Everyone who is NOT to go with you to your destiny will begin to disappear; release them. Yes, it hurts but it will be okay; it's a process towards walking in the will of God for your life.**

- You begin to ask God, "What did Iou do wrong? Are You punishing me and my family? Is my past coming back to haunt me? Is this a generational curse?"

VERY IMPORTANT:

Read 1 Peter 4:12-19 12Beloved, think it not strange concerning
the fiery trial which is to try you, as though some strange thing
happened unto you: 13But rejoice, inasmuch as ye are partakers of
Christ's sufferings; that, when his glory shall be revealed, ye may
be glad also with exceeding joy. 14If ye be reproached for the name
of Christ, happy *are ye*; for the spirit of glory and of God resteth
upon you: on their part he is evil spoken of, but on your part he is
glorified. 15But let none of you suffer as a murderer, or *as* a thief,
or *as* an evildoer, or as a busybody in other men's matters. 16Yet

if *any man suffer* as a Christian, let him not be ashamed; but let
him glorify God on this behalf. 17For the time *is come* that
judgment must begin at the house of God: and if *it* first *begin* at us,
what shall the end *be* of them that obey not the gospel of God?
18And if the righteous scarcely be saved, where shall the ungodly
and the sinner appear? 19Wherefore let them that suffer according
to the will of God commit the keeping of their souls *to him* in well
doing, as unto a faithful Creator.

- Examine your life to make sure this is not a seed you have sown and you are reaping its harvest. If that is the case, then repent and ask God for forgiveness.

- If you have not sown such seeds, then rejoice and know that God is preparing you for a new season of your life and your situation will be a testimony to others.

Season Two Action: What Do You Do?

- Praise and worship God; rejoice because it's your training ground. If you have been a good student and not a rebellious one, graduation season will come soon. If you have been rebellious, you will repeat this season until you have gotten it. Praise and worship God in your mess. Meditate upon His word. You have to exercise faith and know that this season will pass, so ask God what are you to learn and be submissive to the process.

- Your relationship with God will strengthen **IF** you remain in a prayer, thanksgiving, praise, worship and meditating on His word. You will experience another realm of worship. You are now building your faith and relationship with God. Communicate with the Holy Spirit and allow Him to lead you.

- Pray individually and as a family unit. If you pray while you have bitterness and unforgiveness in your heart with anyone, God will not hear your prayer. Forgive everyone who has hurt you. The bitterness and unforgiveness is cancerous; we will discuss in the next chapter.

- Continue to give your tithes and offerings. Sow financial and talent seeds. Yes, you might not have enough money to pay your bills BUT if you honor God first, all your needs will be met. This is a good time to sow financial seed.

- Be submissive to the process. The longer you take to learn, the longer the process will be.

- There is no quick solution – Say, "Have your way Lord" and pray for God's grace, mercy and favor to manifest through you during this process.

- Be positive; do not curse your situation. Remember, life and death is in the power of your tongue. Whatever you speak will manifest in your life. Speak what you want to manifest in your life, not what you are experiencing.

- Husbands and wives are more successful if they pray together. Pray with your children because there is more power in the family unit.

- You should not look like the challenges you are going through. Stay positive. Think positive.

- Stop telling everyone about your challenges unless you are spiritually led to give your testimonies.

- God is weaning you from one season of your life to another season of greatness; stay positive even if you have to cry and praise Him while hurting.

- Know that when God takes something from you, He will replace it with something better. When a mother stops breastfeeding a child, the child will cry but the mother develops "tough love" and withstands the crying baby and introduces a cup to the child. Yes, not knowing the benefit of the cup at first, the child will cry until they realize this is better than what they had before. Likewise, God knows that your future will be better than what you have now. We all have to go through the training process; some of us will not graduate or be promoted because of our attitude. Our attitude is what helps us to determine our latitude and how far God will take us in life. Do we really trust God? We have to understand that nothing happens to us in life unless God approves it. If He approves this mess I am going through, that means He will use it for my good.

Season Three: Promotion/New Beginning

"There is light at the end of the Tunnel" You are beginning to see signs of positive transition in your situation.

- Your blessings are beginning to manifest.

- You are having victory over your challenges.

- Your faith is now stronger.

- You look around your inner circle and it's much smaller.

- You begin to testify on another level of faith.

- You love God more than material things.
- You are more humble and more submissive to God.
- You die to self. You operate on a higher level in the spiritual realm. You are in total surrender to God.
- Material things don't matter anymore.
- The Holy Spirit is your guide. You know and understand the voice of God more now than ever before.
- You and your family love God now more than ever before.
- You pray, praise and worship God on a more intimate level now.

Season Three Action: What Do You Do?

- Continue to praise and worship God.
- Be a mentor to someone. Be reminded that God blesses us so that we can be a blessing to others.
- Do not go back to the relationships that ended; embrace the new ones God is allowing into your life.
- Continue to sow seeds of labor and money. Continue tithing and giving your offering.
- Continue to build on your relationship with God through meditating on His word, fasting, thanksgiving, praise and worship.
- Share your testimonies, as this will help someone from giving up on God's will for their life.

- Continue to develop yourself. Attend seminars and classes according to your gifting and area of influence. Honor your mentors and prayer partners that stood with you through the storm.

In addition to the different stages in life, there are other areas of life we have to be very conscious of if we are experiencing repeated negative results.

Some Common Spiritual Road Blocks that Cause Failure in Life:

- **Cursed Objects**
  - God warns us that bringing a cursed object into our home can bring a curse upon us as well. Deuteronomy 7:26 [26]Neither shalt thou bring an abomination into thine house, lest thou be a cursed thing like it: *but* thou shalt utterly detest it, and thou shalt utterly abhor it; for it *is* a cursed thing.

- **Residing Spirits**
  - Demons are often behind depression, arthritis, cancer, mental illness, fear, seizures, diabetes, etc. Do not own sicknesses. Jesus died for us and by His stripes, we are HEAL**ED** - Isaiah 53:5. You are already healed. You have to claim your healing and speak it over your life. Life and death is in the power of your tongue. After you have examined your heart and know that there is no unforgiveness there, then pray, curse the sickness, reject the sickness and thank Jesus that you are healed.

- **Unpronounced Vows**
  - Vows and oaths bind the soul - Numbers 30:2-9. To break free from ungodly vows, repent of it and renounce it verbally IN JESUS' NAME.
- **Ungodly Soul Ties**
  - Being joined to another person with an unclean spirit can allow transference of bondage and spirits between individuals.
- **Unconfessed Sins**
  - If we confess and repent our sins, God will forgive us - 1 John 1-9.
- **Grudges, Unforgiveness, Bitterness**
  - If you don't forgive others, God will not forgive you - Matthew 6:14-16.
- **Not Willing or Ready for Deliverance**
  - Individuals are not willing or ready to take the necessary steps toward their deliverance.
- **Strongholds**
  - Incorrect thinking pattern. If you see yourself as failure, you will be a failure. Speak the word of God over your life and your loved ones' lives. Life and death is in the power of your tongue - Proverbs 18:21.

- **Dishonoring Your Leaders**
  - Dishonoring parents or people having authority over you (for example, your pastor, teacher or husband), can cause a curse over your life. Hebrews 13:17 [17] Obey them that have the rule over you, and submit yourselves: for they watch for your souls, as they that must give account, that they may do it with joy, and not with grief: for that is unprofitable for you.
- **Lack of Faith**
  - Not understanding or believing God's will about your situation and life – Hebrews 11:1, 6.
- **Trusting in men more than God can cause the Holy Spirit to leave our presence.**
- **Being unjust to the weak, widow, elderly and poor.**
  - Proverbs 21:13 KJV [13]Whoso stoppeth his ears at the cry of the poor, he also shall cry himself, but shall not be heard.
- **Not giving your tithes and offering to the store house of God**
  - (Malachi 3: 8:15) will block the security of your financial blessings.
- **Soulish Prayers**
  - Not praying the will of God. For example, praying for match-making which is not of God.

- **Self-Imposed Curse**
  - Speaking negative things over your life. For example: I am ugly, sick and any words you have spoken over your life that is not aligned with the word of God is placing curses on yourself.

<u>Self-Deliverance</u>

Praying for ourselves to be free from some of these issues can be very difficult if we are not familiar with deliverance ministries. Below, I have summarized how to pray for ourselves and do self-deliverance.

<u>Deliverance is a Process</u>

1. Praise and worship God.
2. Confess scriptures like Luke 10:19 and Psalm 91:3.
3. Say, "I break and renounce all operations of the enemy in my life.
   a. I will give no place to the devil to operate in my life.
   b. My body is the temple of the Holy Spirit.
   c. My mind belongs to God.
   d. My emotions belong to God.
   e. In the name of Jesus, I repent and turn away from all rebellion, hurt, depression, disobedience and unforgiveness. I close any doors I may have open for the enemy to come in. In the name of Jesus, I renounce all works of darkness. I renounce rejection, I renounce unforgiveness, I renounce rebellion, I renounce pride, I renounce bitterness and I renounce poverty in the name of Jesus. Satan you cannot operate in my life. Any spirit of the

enemy operating in my life I command you to leave now in the mighty name of Jesus. Evil spirit, I reject you in the mighty name of Jesus. Every curse operating in my life let your power be released by fire and by force in the name of Jesus. I belong to God and in the power of the Holy Ghost and in the name of Jesus, I command all evil spirits to leave me now. Hallelujah!!! Hallelujah!!! Hallelujah!!!"

4. Put your right hand on your head and left hand on your stomach and say repeatedly, "Holy Ghost fire, burn me from the top of my head to the sole of my feet now in the mighty name of Jesus. When the "Holy Ghost Fire" burns you it's removing any and everything that in your life that is not of God, i.e. sicknesses, diseases, spirits, etc.
5. **Say**, "I saturate myself with the blood of Jesus. Blood of Jesus, enter my spirit, soul and body in the mighty name of Jesus."
6. **Say**, "In the name of Jesus, I cast out you spirit of poverty, infirmity … (Insert whatever spirit that is attacking you) in my life in the name of Jesus."
7. Open your mouth breath in and out several times. If you begin to sneeze, yawn, cough, expel flatulence, know that your prayer is working.
8. Pray in your spiritual language if you have one. If not just call on the name of Jesus.
9. Praise God and thank Him for what He is doing.
10. **Continuous:** Every night, read Psalm 51:1-3, 10.
11. **Continuous:** Every night before you go to bed, pray the following prayer points:
    a. Wall of fire of God, surround me in the name of Jesus

b. I cover myself and my family with the blood of Jesus
c. Angels of God, surround me and my family in the mighty name of Jesus

Additional

Play prophetic soaking music (Musics that expresses God's greatness, power and anointing) in your house all day and all night.

Repent every time you catch yourself saying and doing something that is not agreement with the word of God.

Note for stubborn deliverance: Do a fasting from food. When you fast, you humble your soul and break up soulish things. If your church does not do deliverance, pray and ask the Holy Spirit to lead you to a deliverance ministry where you can get further deliverance help.

Daily Check Point for God to Manifest More in Our Life

- Hebrew 11:1-20 to continue strengthening your faith.
- **Pure Heart**
  - Read Psalm 51 daily and ask God to forgive you of all your sins. As the Holy Spirit to reveal to you any unforgiveness in your heart - Psalm 24:1-10; Matt 5:8. Pray and ask God to reveal to you who you need to forgive today and if there is any hidden unforgiveness in your heart
- **Attitude**
  - Read Psalm 19-12-14 and Psalm 51:12. Be repentive of your sins.

- **Our Mouth is a Weapon**
  - Be slow to speak and quick to listen - James 1:19; Proverbs 18:21. Stay away from gossip. Life and death is in the power of your tongue. Be careful of what you are speaking over your life, your family, your ministry, your business and your surroundigs.
- Every time you open your mouth to speak, angels are recording what you are saying. You are activating angelic forces to work on your behalf. Let your words be positive. Speak to your future, not to your circumstances with no doubt or fear, but life, happiness and success.
- **Listening, Hearing and Acting upon God's Command**
  - My sheep know my voice. John 10:27
  - When God tells us to do something, sometimes it might not makes sense. BUT remember, our blessings are in our obedience. He is our creator; He knows what he created us for. Everything He tells us to do is a line with His will for our life.
- **Renewing our Mind**
  - Your thoughts are very powerfu. Everything that manifests in your life comes from your thoughts. You have the power to change what you think if it does not align with the will and word of God for your life. Create positive thoughts.

Prayer Points for Success

- In the name of Jesus, I confess, renounce and repent of all my sins.
- Lord, forgive me of all my sins. Forgive my children and my spouse of all their sins.
- I call forth a revival in my personal life and in my family in the name of Jesus.
- I forgive all those who have hurt or sinned against me.
- I cover my family, our positions and myself with the blood of Jesus.
- I command all impediments to my destiny to be removed and I bind every hindering spirit in the name of Jesus!
- I loose confusion against every satanic and demonic conspiracy against my life and the life of my family members.
- I terminate every journey into bondage and unfruitfulness designed for me and my family in the name of Jesus.
- No weapon formed against me shall prosper, and every tongue that rises against me in judgment I condemn.
- I shall decree a thing and it shall be established in my life.
- In the name of Jesus, I declare God to be first in my life. God you have priority over all things concerning me and my family.

- I decree and declare this season to be of divine establishment for me, my family, my business and my ministry.

- I speak prosperity in the life of my pastor and his/her family in the name of Jesus.

- I call for every area of my life to come into alignment with God's will.

- We will take possession of our promises in the name of Jesus.

- I command doors of opportunity and elevation to be opened, and I command doors of lack and struggle to be shut permanently now, in the name of Jesus.

- I retrieve all stolen virtues, goodness and blessings in Jesus name.

- In the name of Jesus, I command all satanic agents and devices to be uncovered and removed from my church, my city, my state, my country, my work and my home.

- I command all satanic forecasts spoken against me, my church and family to be nullified and of no effect. Let the counsel of the devil against me be destroyed and frustrated in the name of Jesus.

- I pray for heightened sensitivity to the Holy Spirit. I purpose to hear well and to see clearer in the name of Jesus.

- Open my eyes Lord and let not my ways be darkened before me in the name of Jesus.

- Let the angels of the living God roll away all stones blocking my financial, physical and spiritual breakthrough in the name of Jesus!
- It is a turnaround season for me, my church, my family and my destiny! I return to ruling and reigning for His glory and prevail in all things!!! In the name of Jesus.
- Father, release a spiritual hunger in me to get in Your presence.
- Pour out your Spirit upon me, oh God.
- Bless me indeed and enlarge my coast. Let Your hand be with me and keep me from evil, oh God.
- Oh Lord, let my faith grow exceedingly.
- I am complete in Christ.
- I have the mind of Christ.
- I have a creative mind and I will use it to glorify God.
- I have victory through Christ.

For the next seven days, complete the following exercise honestly. Do not adjust your habits so that this exercise will look good on paper. You are the only person who will see it. Once you have completed the exercise, take a few minutes to carefully examine how your time is spent. Please be reminded that your rest is as important as your work habit and your time with God is by far the most important. He will direct your path as you spend time in His presence.

My Time Spent Per 24 Hours - 2nd Exercise						
	TV/ Internet	Family/ Work	Self / Exercise	Praying/ Meditating on God Word	Sleep	
Monday	2 hours/3 hours	1 hours /11 hours	30 minutes/ 20 minutes	10 minutes	6 hours	24 Hours
Tuesday						24 Hours
Wednesday						24 Hours
Thursday						24 Hours
Friday						24 Hours
Saturday						24 Hours
Sunday						24 Hours

Chapter Notes

Chapter To-Do List

Chapter Four

God Speaks to Us Through Dreams and Visions

Upon completion of my classes, I would lay prostrate and ask God how I did with that specific group I had just finished teaching. I would often ask the Holy Spirit if I missed anything and what I can do to make the next class better. This specific session, the Holy Spirit said, “I am speaking to My people but they are ignoring Me.” I chuckled to myself with amazement and said, “Daddy,” (name I call my God) “we all want to hear from You. What do you mean?” The Holy Spirit responded, “They don’t know it’s Me speaking to them in dreams and visions.” Immediately I said, “Teach me how to help them understand and know it’s You talking to them. I will teach them, Lord.” A hunger arose in me to know more about dreams and visions. I fasted and prayed for God not only to teach me how to teach His people how to pay attention to their dreams and visions, but also how to hear His voice. I also prayed for God to increase my dreams and visions relationship with Him. I had always gotten dreams and visions from God. In fact, most of my dreams would come to past, so I know the importance of paying attention to dreams and visions.

Almost immediately, I began to dream more. Some nights, I would have anywhere from four to five dreams. I would be awakening when I have each scene. I would write it down, go back to sleep and be able to have another dream connected to the first dream. I had no problem at all remembering my dreams. I now became totally devoted to understanding and learning more about dreams, visions and hearing the voice of God. I had a hunger how to get the interpretation. I read all the scriptures in the bible that deal with dreams and visions. I discovered that one-third of the bible is about dreams and visions. I discovered that God did nothing by surprise.

He always warns us, either through dreams and visions, speaking to our spirits, speaking through our pastors, a message or a prophet. God also confirms what He is saying to us. I discovered that in Job 33:14 For God speaketh once, yea twice, *yet man* perceiveth it not, in Acts 2:17 [17] And it shall come to pass in the last days, saith God, I will pour out of my Spirit upon all flesh: and your sons and your daughters shall prophesy, and your young men shall see visions, and your old men shall dream dreams.

Approximately one year later, I had my first dreams and visions workshop. As I prayed for students who believed that they were not dreaming, they began to have dreams and visions. The students in this class requested a part two to this session. They were so intrigued at what God was doing in their life. One of my students had a vision on what she was supposed to name her business. Others had dreams relevant to their businesses and family life.

In this chapter, I will talk about the importance of paying attention to your dreams, visions and much more.

Is God Speaking to Us Through Our Dreams and Visions?

What are the Differences between Dreams and Visions?

What is a Vision?

- God revealing the nature of Himself and we are responding and or communicating with God. Visions are much clearer than dreams.

- Numbers 12:6 KJV [6]And he said, Hear now my words: If there be a prophet among you I the LORD will make myself known unto him in a vision, *and* will speak unto him in a dream.

What is a Dream?

- God revealing His plans and purpose for our life in a sequence of images passing through a sleeping person's mind. Dreams are symbolic.

How to Strengthen Your Communications with God Through Dreams and Visions:

A. Pray and ask God to speak to you through dreams and visions as you sleep.

B. Ask God's forgiveness because you had ignored Him all the years He has been speaking to you.

C. Put a notepad, journal or diary and a pen on your nightstand beside your bed (Office supplies stores have pens that light up at night. This will help you from disturbing your spouse as you record your dreams at night).

D. Title and date your dreams (see sample at end of this chapter).

E. Record the time you were awakened from your dream.

F. Avoid using an alarm clock to wake up when possible because it frightens you out of your sleep and you will forget your dream.

G. Do not fall asleep watching television. The last thing you should do before sleeping is communicate with God.

H. Fall asleep naturally; do not take sleeping pills or alcohol to fall asleep as they can distort your dreams.

I. Try not to eat and fall asleep immediately. Remember, fasting kills the flesh and magnifies your spirit. I find that I dream more and remember my dreams and visions more if I don't eat at least two to three hours before bed time.

J. Say, "I believe in dreams and visions because they're a means of communication from God." What you speak in the atmosphere will manifest. **Job 22:28 [28]Thou shalt also decree a thing and it shall be established unto thee.**

Note: If you usually speak negatively about dreams, then repent and ask God for forgiveness.

Reasons Why We Should Pay Attention to Our Dreams and Visions:

A. God is giving us directions for our businesses, ministries and jobs. Matthew 2:13 KJV [13]And when they were departed, behold, the angel of the Lord appeareth to Joseph in a dream, saying, Arise, and take the young child and his mother, and flee into Egypt, and be thou there until I bring thee word: for Herod will seek the young child to destroy him.

B. God said He would speak to us through dreams and visions. Acts 2:17 KJV [17]And it shall come to pass in the last days, saith God, I will pour out of my Spirit upon all flesh: and your sons and your daughters shall prophesy, and your young men shall see visions, and your old men shall dream dreams.

C. God counsels us at night. Psalm 16:7 KJV I will bless the LORD, who hath given me counsel: my reins also instruct me in the night seasons.

D. God gives us warning dreams when we are not living His will for our life,warning dreams so we can correct our path. Job 33:14-15 [14]For God speaketh once, yea twice, *yet man* perceiveth it not. [15]In a dream, in a vision of the night, when deep sleep falleth upon men, in slumberings upon the bed.

E. God does very important things in our dreams. He established the Abrahamic Covenant in a dream. Genesis 15:12-13, 18 [12]And when the sun was going down, a deep sleep fell upon Abram; and, lo, an horror of great darkness fell upon him. [13]And he said unto Abram, Know of a surety that thy seed shall be a stranger in a land *that is* not theirs, and shall serve them; and they shall afflict them four hundred years... [18]In the same day the LORD made a covenant with Abram, saying, Unto thy seed have I given this land, from the river of Egypt unto the great river, the river Euphrates.

F. God grants supernatural gifts through dreams. 1 Kings 3:5, 9-13, 15 [5]In Gibeon the LORD appeared to Solomon in a dream by night: and God said, Ask what I shall give thee... [9]Give therefore thy servant an understanding heart to judge thy people, that I may discern between good and bad: for who is able to judge this thy so great a people? [10]And the speech pleased the Lord, that Solomon had asked this thing. [11]And God said unto him, Because thou hast asked this thing, and hast not asked for thyself long life; neither hast asked riches for thyself, nor hast asked the life of thine enemies; but hast asked for thyself understanding to discern judgment; [12]Behold, I have done according to thy words: lo, I have given thee a wise and an understanding heart; so that there was none like thee before thee, neither after thee shall any arise like unto thee. [13]And I have also given thee that which thou hast not asked, both riches, and honour: so that there shall not be any among the kings like unto thee all thy days... [15]And Solomon awoke; and, behold, *it was* a dream. And he came to Jerusalem, and stood before the ark of the covenant of the LORD, and offered up burnt offerings, and offered peace offerings, and made a feast to all his servants.

Two Types of Dreams:

1. **Dreams About Us**

   - Dreams about us are dreams that if we remove ourselves from the dream, it would have no subject and it would not make sense.

2. **Dreams About Others**

   - If you are close to a person, you may dream about them. Matthew 27:17-19 [17]Therefore when they were gathered together, Pilate said unto them, Whom will ye that I release unto you? Barabbas, or Jesus which is called Christ? [18]For he knew that for envy they had delivered him. [19]When he was set down on the judgment seat, his wife sent unto him, saying, Have thou nothing to do with that just man: for I have suffered many things this day in a dream because of him.

   - If you are observing something or someone and you are speaking to them and they can't hear you, chances are the dream is about others and not you.

- Ask God what to do with the information. Maybe you are to pray for the person you are dreaming about and not tell them about the dream.

- Gets conformation from God if you should tell the individual about the dream.

- Caution: If you think about a person or thing too much, you begin to dream about them in a "soulish dream." An example is if you see a man you are attracted to and you begin to think about having a relationship with him, you would eventually begin to dream about him. This is not of God; pray and cancel such dream and ask God for His will to be done.

Ways in Which God Helps Us to Understand Our Dreams:

1. Sometimes as we write down our dreams, God will reveal the meaning. 1 Chronicles 28:19 KJV [19]All *this, said David*, the LORD made me understand in writing by *his* hand upon me, *even* all the works of this pattern.

2. God sometimes reveals the meaning of a dream as we are dreaming.

3. God will sometimes reveal the meaning of our dreams as we mature and are ready for its manifestation in our life.

4. God sometimes simultaneously reveals the meaning of our dreams.

5. God sometimes uses a prophet to interpret our dreams.

<u>Some Basic Principles for Interpreting Dreams:</u>

- What is the date of your dream? Dates could correlate with scriptures in the bible. The Holy Spirit will let you know. It could also serve as a timeframe in which Jesus promises to get something to you. I once had a dream that I was six months pregnant. Exactly three months after that, I gave birth to a new book. I didn't remember the dream until the Holy Spirit reminded me and I went back and read my dream log.
- What is the time you were awakened from your dream? The time you awaken from your dream is very relevant. One day, one of my church sisters was telling me her dream and as I listened to her, the Holy Spirit told me to ask her what was the time of her dream. The Holy Spirit then told me what book of the bible to look in. As I read the hour representing the chapter and the minute representing the verse representing when she was awakened from her dream, it was identical to the dream she had (example: 12:15am would be Genesis 12:15 or any chapter in the bible that has a 12th chapter and a 15th verse). We both were amazed and started to praise God. The Holy Spirit revealed to us that it was a prophetic dream and confirmed it in the bible.
- What was your emotion during the dream? Were you scared or happy?
- What was your action during the dream? Were you falling, flying or running?
- What were the symbols in your dream? Symbols may come from your life or your surroundings. Genesis 37:5-7 KJV
  [5]And Joseph dreamed a dream, and he told *it* his brethren: and they hated him yet the more. [6]And he said unto them,

Hear, I pray you, this dream which I have dreamed: [7]For, behold, we *were* binding sheaves in the field, and, lo, my sheaf arose, and also stood upright; and, behold, your sheaves stood round about, and made obeisance to my sheaf.

Symbols in Our Dreams:

A. **Numbers:** Are literal (Genesis 40:8) and may be interpreted as a precise message.

B. **People**

   A. A person's name, especially if it's spoken in the dream is very significant. What's the meaning of the name?

   B. Seeing other people that you are close to represents parts of yourself

      A. Family members or friends - What's their dominant character?

      B. Police – Represent authority

C. **Jesus and Angels**

   A. If Jesus or the angel speaks to you in a dream or vision, it is literal

D. **Colors**

   A. **Positive Brown:** compassion, pastor, humility; **Negative Brown: d**ead, tired, humanism

B. **Positive Red:** prophetic anointing, wisdom, anointing power; **Negative Red:** anger, bloodshed, war

C. **Positive Purple:** royalty, authority, kingship, apostle

D. **Positive White:** Spirit of the Lord, holy power, purity**;** **Negative White:** religious spirit

E. **Animal Emotions**

   A. Horse - authority, power

   B. Bull - anger, spiritual warfare, persecution

   C. Cat - independent thinking, curiosity, self-willed

   D. Fox - crafty, cunning,

   E. Lion - loyalty, dominion, bold, power

House - represents the person; their life; one's spiritual state. (Matthew 7:24-27; 2 Timothy 2:20-21)

A. **House, discovering a new room within -** If associated with positive feelings: New area of life or ministry God will open or desires to open if you'll cooperate with Him. If associated with negative feelings: A dark part of your life the Lord wants to expose and or heal.
B. **House that's torn or dilapidated** - Signifies a lack of spiritual covering; having an area of life in which God's protection has been withdrawn due to sin or an upcoming wrong choice.

C. **Nakedness** - Represents intimacy with God. Standing naked before God represents surrender to God (Genesis 3:8-11) and or transparency of one's self. Also, means the person will be transparent or vulnerable.

D. **Dream of someone dying**- If you don't see any blood it could mean a career, a relationship or something in the person's life is coming to an end.

E. **Vehicles** - Represents the current path or direction of one's life due to decisions made.

   a. **Car-** Personal path, individual ministry.

   b. **Multi-passenger (buses, trains, etc.)** - Same as above but involving a group of people such as one's family, corporation, church, denomination or movement. A bus wreck with injuries: warning that a specific decision or the current course will lead to bad results for the people involved.

F. **Snakes, serpents** - Represents the enemy; demons; a bad omen; danger (Genesis 3:1; Numbers 21:4-9).

G. **Water, rushing or fast flowing** - If associated with a positive feeling: indicates the blessing of God; the presence of the Holy Spirit (Ezekiel 47:1-9).

H. **Dreams of losing your purse** - God is communicating that the dreamer has lost or is looking for his or her purpose, identity and favor.

I. **Dreams about storms** - If the color of the storm is white/light, it's a move from God. If the color is black or dark, it's a destructive force from the power of darkness.

J. **Dream of having sexual intercourse** (spiritual husband) - Seek a prophetic ministry for deliverance help. Pray and ask the Holy Spirit to lead you a true prophetic ministry.

K. **Dreams of being injected** - Seek a prophetic ministry for deliverance help. Pray and ask the Holy Spirit to lead you a true prophetic ministry.

Important Things About Dreams and Visions

A. One third of the bible is about dreams and visions. God is giving His people instructions, gifts, warnings and or encouragements in our dreams as we sleep.

B. Sin, trials, dream illiteracy and competing voices can cause us not to remember our dreams.

C. Scientifically, we dream five to seven dreams per night.

D. When you have a recurring dream, it's because you are not paying attention to what the dream is telling you; therefore, you should pray and ask the Holy Spirit to reveal the meaning and direction as to what you are to do.

E. The dreamer's heart will leap and witness to the interpretation of a dream.

    A. Never interpret a dreamer's dream; we may offer suggestions as to what it means. Remember, a dream will never counteract the word of God.

F. Always remember that you should pray and ask God for the interpretation of your dream if you are not sure what it means, because dream interpretation comes from God.

G. Your dreams are calling you to act, so pay attention and pray accordingly.

H. Warning dreams are conditional. If you pray and ask for repentance from the path you are taking and change your action, then God can deliver you.

I. Create a Symbol Chart for yourself. For example, when I dream of my dad, it's God speaking to me, and my mom literally represents me.

J. If you are not sure what a dream means, pray and ask God to help your understanding.

K. A stranger in your dream could represent an angel or a demon. Were you fearful of the stranger? If yes, it could be a demon. Even if you did not know the person but you felt relaxed and comfortable in their presence, chances are it's an angel protecting you or giving you a message.

L. If you are forgetting your dreams, read Psalm 27 prior to going to bed; pray and ask the Holy Spirit to give you total recall of your dreams and visions according to the will of God.

Note: Always thank God for speaking to you through dreams and visions. Thank God for revelations and the interpretation of your dreams.

Visions:

Visions Come as a Turning Point in Our Life:

A vision is God revealing the nature of Himself, and we are responding and or communicating with God. Visions are much clearer that dreams.

- **Five Keys for Your Visions to Manifest:**

    1. You must pray to activate it. A lot of us believe when we get a prophetic word it will automatically come to pass. Remember, when a prophetic word is given, two forces heard it: the demonic forces and the angelic forces. The devil does not want to see us prosper or live God's will for our life. The devil is here to steal, kill and destroy; therefore, we have to pray and protect our prophetic word.

    2. Wait for God to reveal it to you.

    3. Act upon what God shows you. Begin to prepare yourself. Example, if He tells you that you will have a successful restaurant, begin to study successful restaurant habits. Research the required documents you will need to start a restaurant. Examine why one failed so you don't make the same mistake.

    4. Let God fulfill it in His time. Remember, God's timing is perfect. If you begin to have doubt, you are in actuality saying you don't trust God's word. Do not mummer. Praise and worship God as you wait for Him to fulfill His promises.

5. Don't lose faith if you believe it has been delayed. Hebrews 11:6 [6]But without faith *it is* impossible to please *him*: for he that cometh to God must believe that he is, and *that* he is a rewarded of them that diligently seek him.

Call to Action Excercise

Don't live in sin and expect your visions from God to manifest:

We have a role to play in the manifestation of our dreams and visions:

- Maintain consistency in your prayer life.

- Praise and worship God.

- When you pray, be still and quiet for a moment to hear what God's response is.

    - Remember, prayer is a two-way conversation between you and God.
    - Prayer is one of the ways we release the will of God upon the earth.
    - Prayer is earthly license for heavenly interference.
    - Prayer is not an option for believers.
    - Prayer is a way of life for believers.
    - Prayer plugs us in the power source of the supernatural realm.
    - Prayer is the legal authority to dominate earth.
    - Prayer is man giving God permission to interfere in earths' affairs.
    - Prayer also helps us walk perfectly and completely in the will of God.

    - Praying and confessing the word of God is realizing the mind of God.

- There will be no victory without a fight, so stay focused on the promises of God.
- Purchase a composition notebook and a pen that lights up when your write. Have your notepad and pen on your nightstand. God will also speak to you sometimes while you are worshiping Him and meditating on His word. Be ready to write when He says write.
- Pray and ask God to help you to remember your dreams.

Chapter Notes

Chapter To-Do List

Chapter Five

Transitioning Into Who You Are Created to Be

Ask yourself the following questions. If your responses are yes, then you are on the right track:

- Can I use my gifts and talents in this new career, business or ministry?
- Do I enjoy performing the duties in this new career, business or ministry?
- Has God communicated with me regarding this venture?
- Would I perform the activities in this ministry, career or business for free?
- Do I have a passion for this career, ministry or business?

Meet with your immediate family members to communicate your business venture and solicit their help.

Family members can help you with your new venture in the following areas if the Holy Spirit has not yet revealed them to you. One of my students got the name of her business in a dream. God will sometimes reveal things about your business ministry or career to others.

- Suggest names for your new business.
- Suggest logos for your new business.
- Suggest mission statements for your new business.
- Your children can research similar businesses on the Internet and report their findings on business or ministry practices, their strengths and weaknesses.

- Schedule a time to meet with family members to discuss progress.
- Do not schedule meetings during times when other family members have previous engagements (they may develop a resentment towards your mission).
- Pray before and after each meeting. Express gratitude toward each family member for their help.
- Meeting days and times should be agreed upon by all members.
- Allow each family member to report their assignment results without criticizing their effort.
- Be positive and honest about each member's feedback.

New Venture Test

To help you determine what business to start, ask yourself the following questions:

1. What do I enjoy doing?

2. What do I enjoy doing that I would do for free?

3. What do I do well?

4. What do I perform effortlessly while others struggle to do it?

5. What is God's will for my life? What is the Holy Spirit prompting me to do?

Note: Your number one reason for starting a business or a ministry should not be to make money. Yes, it sounds ironic but it's true. If you focus on the money, you can lose the quality of service or product. You will not have the joy, peace and passion as you complete your day-to-day tasks. Yes, you should monitor your business profit line. You should have the best accounting personnel. But it should not be your vocal point of interest. In other words, don't start a business because of how much money you can make; rather, the driving force should be that it's your passion and God's will for your life. If these two components are in place, the grace, mercy and favor of God will manifest greatly in your life and business or ministry. Because you are doing what you are created to do, you will enjoy life. As you focus on building your business and or ministry with your passion being the driving force, your profit line will be incredible.

Your assignment in life is in your uniqueness; embrace it, nourish it and cherish it. Once you have determined what it is that God created you to do, then it's time for you to make note of the following:

- **Be clear on <u>WHY</u> you want to start this career, business or ministry**
- **Be clear on <u>WHOM</u> you want to do business or ministry with**
- **Be clear on <u>WHAT</u> type of career, business or ministry you want to start**
- **Be clear on <u>WHEN</u> you want to start this business, ministry or career**
- **Be clear on <u>WHERE</u> you want to start this business, ministry, or career**

<u>Call to Action Excercise Exercise</u>

- Your blessings are dependent on your willingness to push through your struggles.

- A family that prays together, stays together. Have prayer time with your family.

- Satan attacks those in line for a blessing. Your attack is usually because of the blessings in front of you. The attack is supposed to detour you and keep distracted. But if you are in relationship with God, He will warn you before you encounter it, maybe through dreams, visions, a prophet, your spiritual leader or while communing with Him. There is no limit as to how God will communicate with us; pray for a stronger spirit of discernment so you will not miss when He is speaking to you. Sometimes situations we go through are a part of our process for God's will to manifest in our life. Nothing will happen to us unless God allows it. If God allows it, it will be used for His glory. Remember, Jesus warned Peter that Satan has asked to sift all of him as wheat (Luke 22:31). Satan has to get permission from God to touch us, so know that everything happening in your life will ultimately be used to glorify God. Yes, sometimes we allow access by sinning.

- Pray for what you want versus what you don't want. You will magnify what you focus on in your life. Focus on the positive.

- Speak blessings over yourself and your family everyday. Life and death is in your mouth. Create positive things with your mouth.

- STOP COMPLAINING! Instead ask God what are you supposed to learn from the situation or challenges you are encountering.

- Every situation is God-used but not God-sent. Your situation will be used to develop you. It's training ground. The quicker you pass the test, the faster your promotion will come. Remember, when the student is taking a test, the teacher is quiet. If you believe God is not responding to you and you are living right, chances are that you are taking a test. Praise and worship Him with the tears in your eyes, knowing that this season will pass. "Only salvation is lasting."

- Success is in your differences and your uniqueness. Love yourself. Look in the mirror each morning and say something positive to yourself; stop waiting on people to speak positive things into your life.

- Luke 6:38 [38]Give, and it shall be given unto you; good measure, pressed down, and shaken together, and running over, shall men give into your bosom. For with the same measure that ye mete withal it shall be measured to you. Sow financial seed. The seasons of your life will change every time you decide to use your faith.

- The seed you sow is the seed you will reap bountifully. Do well unto others on purpose.

- Be respectful and obedient to your leaders.

- What you feed grows and what you starve dies. Feed your relationship with God.

- How long did you spend with your family today? Have you told them and showed them that you love them?

- How long did you spend gossiping or on social media today? Make sure you spend more time with God.

- How long did you spend praying and worshiping God today? Have you told God lately that you love Him? Have you told Him thanks for the air you breathe? Have you told Him thanks that you can walk, eat, see and talk?

- How long did you spend watching TV today?

Invest in your mind, your family, future and most importantly, your relationship with God, and you will have a prosperous life.

Final Section Prayer:

Prayer Points

1. We bless you, Lord.
2. We praise, honor and adore you, Lord.
3. We thank you for life, grace, mercy and favor.
4. We thank you for our family and friends.
5. We thank you for good health.
6. We thank you for the air we breathe.
7. We thank you for our jobs and business.
8. We thank you for creative minds.
9. We thank you for the anointing to do business.
10. We thank you for the anointing to start and maintain this new venture.
11. We thank you for the "stuff" you have blessed us with.
12. Thank you, God. Thank you, Jesus. Thank you, Holy Spirit.
13. Thank you for wisdom and knowledge on how to proceed with this new venture.
14. We thank you for your protection and guidance through this process.
15. Lord, forgive me of my sins. Wash me and cleanse me, oh Lord.

a. Forgive my children of their sins
b. Forgive my family of their sins
c. Forgive my nation of its sins

16. Lord, remove every spirit of offense in me. I choose to release offense in the name of Jesus because I know you cannot bless me fully if I keep offenses in my heart.
17. Lord, help me to keep my heart pure.
18. Fire of God. purify anything in me that is not of God.
19. Fire of God, purify my mind, soul and body.
20. Help me to operate in the spirit of excellence, oh God.
21. Lord, remove everyone in my life who is a hindrance to your will for my life.
22. Lord, show us your mercy.
23. Let your mercy manifest in my life, in my businesses, in my school, in my job and in my church in the name of Jesus.
24. Lord, have your way in my life, the life of my children, spouse and church members in the name of Jesus.
25. Let there be a positive shifting in my life, family and church in the mighty name of Jesus.
26. Oh God, we thank you for Jesus our Lord, savior and deliverer.
27. As your word said in Acts 2:17, pour out your spirit upon me, oh God.
28. We call forth revival in our life, nation, church and home.
29. Revive us, oh God.
30. Your word in Matthew 7:7 says ask and it shall be done. We are asking, oh God, for a visitation from you. Visit us in our dreams and visions, in the market places, in the schools and on our jobs.
31. Holy Ghost fire burn away anything and everything in my life that is not of you, God.

32. We want more of you, Lord.
33. Hear our cry, oh God.
34. Give us a hunger for your word, Lord.
35. We want to see you more.
36. We want to see you more.
37. We want to hear you more.
38. We want to feel you more.
39. We want to feel your presence.
40. Lord, we need more of you.
41. I cover my family , my church, my ministry, my businesses and myself with the blood of Jesus.
42. We cover our spouses and children with the blood of Jesus.
43. We cover our possessions with the blood of Jesus.
44. I release the blood of Jesus to wipe away every injustice in my life in the mighty of Jesus.
45. Lord, release a spirit of boldness in me to do your will in my life.
46. Lord, help us to pay our tithes and offerings and to sow seeds.
47. I pull down every stronghold over our mind that would block the flow of God in our life.
48. I brake out of demonic limitations.
49. Lord, free me from the stronghold of my enemies and of my mind in the name of Jesus.
50. I rebuke the spirit of slumber and procrastination from my life in the mighty name of Jesus.
51. I rebuke the spirit of death over my life and I speak life more abundantly.
52. We decree and declare the evil one has no place in our heart in the mighty name of Jesus.
53. Lord, we thank you for divine positioning.
54. Lord, we thank you for divine provision.

55. Lord, we thank you for divine turnaround in our life.
56. Lord, we thank you for divine favor.
57. Lord, we thank you for divine connections.
58. Lord, we thank you for supernatural supply and blessings.
59. Lord, we thank you for financial breakthrough.
60. As sons and daughters of the most high God, we thank you that we have the best life has to offer (spectacular cars and homes).
61. Help us to understand what's on your heart and your mind, Lord, and help us to be a good steward of it.
62. Holy Spirit, teach us how to touch the heart of my Lord and Savior.
63. Lord, I want more of you.
64. Lord, let us be fully possessed by you.
65. Upgrade our prayer life, Lord.
66. Upgrade our faith, Lord.
67. Upgrade our anointing.
68. Teach me how to pray, Holy Spirit.
69. Let our tongue be loosed to access heaven.
70. Open the eyes my understanding, Lord.
71. Let there be an open Heaven over our life, family, church and businesses.
72. Lord, let there be a supernatural breakthrough for me and my family.
73. I present my body as a living sacrifice; use me for your glory Lord.
74. Let our prayer vocabulary be loosed to access heaven.
75. Let us live in your glory realm.
76. Grant us wisdom how to praise and worship you, Lord.
77. We release ourselves of any stronghold of the enemy.
78. I mute the voice of my enemy.
79. Lord, let us see true power of your angelic forces.

80. Lord, let grace, mercy and favor prevail over us.
81. Free us from limitation, Lord.
82. Reveal yourself to me, Lord.
83. I rebuke the spirit of confusion in my life.
84. I rebuke the spirit of sickness over my life and the life of my love ones.
85. I rebuke the spirit of poverty and I speak prosperity in the mighty name of Jesus.
86. Money will always meet money in my hands in the mighty name of Jesus.
87. I am crowned with wealth (Proverbs 14:24) in the mighty name of Jesus.
88. The Lord is my shepherd and I shall not want (Psalm 23:1-2).
89. Abraham's blessings are mine (Galations 3:14) in the mighty name of Jesus.
90. Wealth and riches are in my house and my righteousness endures forever (Psalm 112:3).
91. Oh heavens over my prosperity, open by fire in the name of Jesus.
92. Oh God, arise and empower me to prosper in the name of Jesus.
93. I have favor with God and man (Luke 2:52).
94. Every power sitting on my wealth, fall down and die in the name of Jesus.
95. Foundational poverty die in the name of Jesus.
96. I am significant and will impact others positively in the name of Jesus.
97. I am an agent of positive change in the mighty name of Jesus.
98. Blood of Jesus flow into my life.
99. My bloodline is purified with the blood of Jesus.

100. Every poison in my bloodline, dry up and die in the name of Jesus.
101. Curses operating in my bloodline, break and dry up in the name of Jesus.
102. My foundation, become fire and receive the fire of God in the name of Jesus.
103. Anything in me that is giving my enemy power, die now in the name of Jesus.
104. Any power assigned to waste my destiny, die in the name of Jesus.
105. Oh God, arise in your mercy and fight my battles.
106. I will not miss the timetable of God for my life in the name of Jesus.
107. God is giving me a dramatic turnaround in my finances (name your struggle).
108. Holy Ghost fire, consume me and consume my foundation now in the mighty name of Jesus.
109. Lord give us dreams and visions of inventive ideas and help us to be good stewards of it.
110. Let all hindering spirits be destroyed in the name of Jesus.
111. Every barrier holding my destiny, be destroyed now in the name of Jesus.
112. Satanic barriers, be removed in the name of Jesus.
113. I lose myself from all evil and evil soulties in the name of Jesus.
114. In the name of Jesus, I will have testimonies this month, in 2015 and years beyond.
115. I decree and declare everything in my life and my children's life will come into divine alignment with God's will for our life.
116. I overcome evil with good.

117. God gives me knowledge and wisdom in all areas where I lack and I am receiving it in the name of Jesus.
118. I will always speak positive things over my life and my children's life in the name of Jesus.
119. All nations and generations call me blessed.
120. I am chosen by God and I am blessed.
121. God is giving me fresh eyes to see opportunities today, and I am seeing them and they will manifest in my life.
122. God is giving me fresh ideas today and I will put into practice every idea He has downloaded today.
123. My spouse, children and I are prosperous in all areas of life.
124. I cover myself, my family and my possessions with the blood of Jesus.
125. I am my own brand.
126. I am anointed for wealth and prosperity.
127. I decree and declare I will lend to many nations and I will not borrow.
128. I decree and declare I am the best in my field.
129. I decree and declare the fire of God is burning every plan of the devil in my life, my children's life and my spouse's life.
130. I arrest every demonic spirit that would try to attack my life and destiny.
131. Let me understand and have revelation of your will and purpose for my life, Lord.
132. Lord, show me the plans that you have for me and my family and how to achieve them.
133. I surrender to your will for my life and the life of my family, oh God.
134. Give me the wisdom and the knowledge how to achieve your will for my life, Lord.

135. Lord, close all doors in my life that need to be closed and open doors that need to be opened in Jesus name, Amen.
136. Thank you, Lord, for divine positioning and provision for my business.
137. Thank you, Lord, for divine connections.
138. Lord, I thank you for answering all my prayers in the name of Jesus, Amen.

With a voice of thanksgiving say Hallelujah!!! seven times (the number seven symbolizes rest).

If you have not received Jesus as your Lord and Savior, say this prayer out loud:

Salvation Prayer

Say this with your heart and lips out loud

Heavenly Father, I come to You in the name of Jesus. Your Word says, 'Whosoever shall call on the name of the Lord shall be saved' (**Acts 2:21**). I am calling on You. I pray and ask Jesus to come into my heart and be Lord over my life. According to **Romans 10:9-10**: 'If thou shalt confess with thy mouth the Lord Jesus, and shalt believe in thine heart that God has raised him from the dead, thou shalt be saved. For with the heart man believeth unto righteousness; and with the mouth confession is made unto salvation.' I do that now. I confess that Jesus is Lord, and I believe in my heart that God raised Him from the dead. I want to trust and follow You as my Lord and Savior in Jesus' name, Amen.

A note from me (Janet Melwani): **As a minister of the gospel** of Jesus Christ, I tell you today that all of your sins are forgiven. Always remember to run to God and not from God because He loves you and has a great plan for your life. Blessings and welcome to your new chapter…

Chapter Notes:

Chapter To-Do List

Section 2

Chapter Six

Business Plan Outline

Writing Your Business Plan:

A business plan is the blueprint of your business. It is your directive tool that establishes the foundation of your business. Schedule uninterrupted time to start writing your business plan. It is very effective if you schedule time to work on this project at the time of day you are most productive. You will be able to focus and think clearly and thoughts will flow easily.

Speak with people, both successful and not so successful, within your line of business. Filter the information you received (use the information that will help your business and disregard any information that's not necessary for the success of your business). Record the best practices of other businesses and note their reasons for failure. This information will be crucial because as you build your business, you can implement your great ideas and not repeat the poor decisions that cause businesses to fail.

Select a business mentor; this should be someone that supports your dream and believes in your success. Don't be in a rush to select a mentor but wait on God's divine direction and He will make the divine connection.

Sample Business Plan

Because your business plan is the blueprint for your business, you should spend quality time working on clearly defining your business model. Use clear and simple language to communicate your ideas and visions. A well written business plan will play a key role in the success of your business. You will also need your business plan for loans and certifications.

Make sure you have a passion for owning the business you plan to start. You should always pray before you start your business plan and schedule uninterrupted time to formulate your ideas. Don't be frustrated if an idea does not flow; just trust God because He is in control. Your ideas for your business will flow when the time is right. Be sure to work on your business plan the time of day when you function the best. If you function best as a "morning person," then schedule uninterrupted time in the morning to start formulating your business plan.

Be willing to solicit ideas from other successful small and large businesses, family members, government agencies and your mentor. Visit your local SCORE chapter and Small Business Administration (SBA) office (www.sba.gov). Learn everything you can about the business you want to establish. Research your business ideas to determine if there is a need for your services or products. Utilize the following sources for gathering statistical and demographical information:

- Internet/Social Media
- Chamber of Commerce
- Libraries and published directories
- Family and friends
- Small Business Administration

Study and evaluate your competitors and keep accurate records of your findings. Test your ideas with potential customers, friends and family members who can offer constructive feedback. Be prepared to make changes to your business plan based on feedback you received after you have validated the information.

Components of a Business Plan

Company Description

- Mission Statement
- Company Goals and Objectives
- Business Philosophy
- Future Plans

Industry Analysis

- Catering /Restaurant Industry
- Future Trends and Strategic Opportunities
- Company Strengths and Core Competencies

Services and Products

- The Menu
- Production
- Services

Target Market

- 3 Major Segments
- Customer Profiles
- Competitive Strategy

Marketing Plan and Strategy

- Market Penetration
- Marketing Strategy
- Marketing Plan
- Effort

Operations

- Employee Training and Education
- System and Controls
- Food Production
- Delivery Service

Management and Organization

- Management Structure
- Ownership
- Milestone
- Risk Evaluation

Appendices

- Menu

Below is a sample of a Business Plan.

Company Description

JGTDXX is a unique family owned and operated Caribbean restaurant with a highly motivated staff and stellar customer service. We provide the most appetizing Caribbean food in Central Florida. Our staff has over 20 years of combined customer service experience in the hospitality and food industry. JGTDXX specializes in blending other cultures with daily delights from around the world and our food specials are the highlight of our theme. We are also current members of several chambers of commerce in the Central Florida area and certified as a Minority and Women Owned Business Enterprise for Orange County.

Mission Statement

- Our company's goal is to focus on the success of the business, the high quality of food, attitude, fairness, understanding and generosity between management, staff, customers and vendors.

- We will promote and develop unity among cultures through food while generating enthusiasm and excitement among each other.

- We will present a variety of dishes to the community that everyone will enjoy and find appetizing. Awareness of all these factors and the responsible actions that result will give our business a sense of purpose and meaning beyond our basic financial goals.

Company's Goals and Objectives

- All JGTDXX employees will take pride in providing our customers with world-class customer service while blessing their appetites with mouth-watering food.

- All team members will model the credo, "***Put God first in everything we do,***" and this means we will conduct business with integrity and treat our customers with the utmost respect.

- JGTDXX will become the most talked about restaurant because of our Christ-like manner, our food and our commitment to high-quality service and community involvement. We will tangibly commit to contribute to the community at large.

Business Philosophy

- Put God first in everything we do and have a passion for what we do

- Have a passion for people and to serve people

- To treat others as we would like to be treated

Target Market Sector

JGTDXX will market to families of all cultures and ethnicities in the surrounding communities. We will also be expanding to other areas, communities and states. The core principle of our business is to ***unite people through food***. We will offer a variety of foods, i.e., Jamaican, Chinese, Italian and American.

Future Plans

When our business meets its overhead projections by our second year, we will start scouting for a second location in the Central Florida area and develop plans for the next restaurant unit. Our six-year goal is to have three restaurants in the Central Florida region and to serve at least four different culturally diverse cuisines.

Industry Analysis

Although the restaurant industry is very competitive, the lifestyle changes created by modern living continue to fuel its steady growth. More and more people have less time, resources and ability to cook for themselves. Trends are very important and JGTDXX is well positioned for the current market for quick meals at moderate to low prices.

The Restaurant Industry Today

I believe the food service business is the third largest industry in the country. It accounts for over $240 billion annually in sales, and the independent restaurant sector accounts for 15% of that total. The average American spends 15% of his/her income on meals away from home. This number is steadily increasing. There are 600 new restaurants opening every month and over 200 more are needed to keep pace with the increasing demand.

At our restaurant, patrons will be able to satisfy their appetites with whatever flavor they so desire, whether it be Jamaican, Chinese, Italian or American cuisine.

Future Trends and Strategic Opportunities

I believe the predicted growth trend is very positive both in short- and long-term projections. People will be compelled to eat more meals away from home because the generation today is working two or more jobs and time does not permit them to cook.

Important Company Strengths and Core Competencies:

- Strengths
  - Cooking ability
  - Interpersonal skills
  - 20 years of hospitality experience
  - 15 years of food service experience
  - Customer service experience
  - Positive relationship with different chambers of commerce
- Core Competencies
  - Food Service
  - Hospitality
  - Customer Service
  - Accounting

Related Services and Products

JGTDXX Restaurant will offer a menu of food and beverages with a distinctive image. There will be four ways to purchase our products: table service at the restaurant, take-out from the restaurant, home or office delivery and at catering events.

The Menu

JGTDXX's menu is moderate in size and moderately-priced. We offer a collection of Jamaican, Chinese, Italian and American cuisine that's flavorful and familiar. Our goal is to create the image of satisfying and nutritious food.

Production

Food production and assembly will take place in the restaurant's kitchen. Fresh vegetables, meat and dairy products are some of the ingredients that will be used to create most of the dishes from scratch. The chef will implement strict standards of sanitation, quality food production and presentation, and/or packaging.

Service

There will be three ways a customer can purchase food. Customers may dine in and be serviced by a waiter or waitress. Customers may also pick up their food at our take-out counter. Most take-out food will be cooked to order with orders coming from via telephone or fax. Delivery service (an indirect form of take-out) will also be available at certain times and to limited areas.

Target Market

The market for JGTDXX's products covers a large area of diverse and heavily populated groups. Our products will be marketed in areas that are surrounded by a lot of human traffic and by other businesses that will direct customers to our restaurant. This is an area where people travel by foot or car to eat out and one that is also frequented by tourists. It is also an area known for and caters to the demographic group we are targeting.

The customer base will come from three major segments:

- Local residents
- Tourists
- Local businesses

The food concept and product image of JGTDXX will attract several different customer profiles:

- Students and Singles
- Single Parents
- Multi-cultural Families
- The Health Conscious
- Food Lovers

Competitive Strategy and Business Philosophy

There are major ways in which we will create an advantage over our competitors:

- Put God first in everything we do and have a passion for what we do.
- Have a passion for people and to serve people
- Treat others as we would like to be treated
- Product identity, branding, quality and uniqueness
- High employee motivation and good sales attitude (everyone is a sales person)

- Innovative and aggressive service options

Market Penetration

Entry into the market should not be a problem. We will utilize pre-opening advertising and public relations campaigns. Also, as CEO, I will be visiting local chambers of commerce, churches, schools, small business organizations and networking events and sending out e-mail blasts.

Marketing Strategy

Because our central focus will be based on the unique aspect of the product theme, "Tasty Foods," a mix of marketing vehicles will be created to convey our presence, our image and our message.

Marketing Plan:

Marketing research

Economics

Products

Features and Benefits

Customers

Competition

Niches

Strategies

Sales Forecast

Consistency is Key in Marketing

Social Media

Internet

Print media - Newspapers, magazines and student publications

Broadcast media - local programming and special interest shows, local radio

Networking - Charity, chamber of commerce events and other professional group

Direct mail - Subscriber lists, offices flyers (repeat every two weeks)

The marketing effort will be split into Three phases:

1) Opening: Flyers to businesses and residences; word-of-mouth.

2) Ongoing: Specials: sales, etc.

3) Point of Sale: A well-trained staff can increase the average check as well as enhance the customer's overall experience. Employee and customer referrals are very important factors in building a strong customer base.

Operations

Employee training and education on our products, services and core values.

Employees will be trained not only in their specific operational duties, but in the philosophy and applications of the overall company concept.

Employees will know the menu ingredient, and will taste test all new items on the menu. All employees are considered our "salesmen."

Systems and Controls

A big emphasis is being placed on extensive research into the quality and integrity of our products. Our products will constantly be tested to maintain our own high standards of freshness and purity. Food costs and inventory control will be tracked by our computer system and reviewed by management for accuracy.

Food Production

Our food will be prepared on company premises. The kitchen will be designed to meet high standards of sanitary efficiency and it will be thoroughly cleaned daily. Our food will be made to order.

Delivery and Catering

Food for delivery may be similar to take-out (prepared to order) or it may be prepared earlier and stocked. If no servers are required, all catering orders will be treated as deliveries.

Management Structure

Janet G ….. President and Chief Operating Officer

Dee G…….. Assistant Chef

Tev G …….. Marketing Director

Geo G ……..Sales Person

Jasmine G……Accountant

Lucia G………. Social Media Specialist

Ownership

Janet G will retain 100 percent ownership.

Long-Term Development

JGTDXX is an innovative concept that targets a new, growing market. We assume that the market will respond and grow quickly in the next five years. Our goals are to create a reputation of quality, consistency and security (food safety) that will make us the leader of a new style of dining.

Strategies

Our marketing efforts will be concentrated on take-out and delivery, the areas of most promising growth. As the market changes, new products may be added to maintain sales and keep up with the growing trends.

Milestones

After the restaurant opens, we will keep a close eye on all sales and profits. Three years later, we will look at expanding the restaurant.

Risk Evaluation

As with any new venture, there is risk involved. The success of our project hinges on the strength and acceptance of a new market. After the first year, we expect some copycat competition in the form of other independent units.

Chapter Assignment

- Exercise at least 25 minutes each day for five days per week.
- Spend quality time with God each day thanking Him for His direction with your new business.
- Start to formulate your business goals and objectives for your business plan.
- Thank God for closing all doors that need to be closed and for opening all doors that need to be opened in your life.
- Embrace your new positive associations.
- Thank God in advance for developing your hearing so you can hear Him speaking to you clearly.
- Celebrate and treat yourself to something you enjoy doing. Pat yourself on the shoulder for your progress.
- Continue sowing seeds with your talents and offerings.
- Give your tithes (10% of all income you receive).
- Read Psalm 1 and Psalm 91 daily.

Chapter Notes

Chapter To-Do List

Chapter Seven

Formulating Your Business

Determine the Legal Structure of Your Business

For this subject matter of determining your business structure, I totally recommend that you consult an accountant. It is important that you consider your tax saving options for your unique business and or non-profit organization. Below are the different types of legal structures one should consider when starting their business or ministry:

- Sole Proprietorship - A business owned and managed by one individual who is personally liable for all business debts and obligations.
- Partnership - A single business owned by two or more people.
- Corporation - A legal entity owned by shareholders.
- S-Corporation - A special type of corporation created through a tax election. An eligible domestic corporation can avoid double taxation (once to the shareholders and again to the corporation) by electing to be treated as an S-corporation.
- Limited Liability Company (LLC) - A hybrid legal structure that provides the limited liability features of a corporation and the tax efficiencies and operational flexibility of a partnership.
- Non-Profit - An organization engaged in activities of public or private interest where making a profit is not a primary

mission. Some non-profits are exempt from paying federal taxes.

- 501(c)(3) - A tax-exempt, non-profit corporation

- Cooperative - A business or organization owned by and operated for the benefit of those using its services. Cooperatives are not a legal structure.

Registering Your Business

- Register your business with the required local, state and federal government
- Determine your corporation structure
- Choose your company business name
- Apply for any required business licenses
- State of Florida: www.sunbiz.org (Apply to your respective state agency); www.myflorida.com
- County: Determine occupational license and zoning requirements depending on your city and county; Florida - www.orangecountyfl.net and/or www.cityoforlando.net
- Taxes: Apply for an Employer Identification Number (www.irs.gov); register with State of Florida (or your respective state) for sales tax - Florida Department of Revenue

Chapter Assignment

- Exercise at least 35 minutes each day for five days per week.
- Spend quality time with God each day, thanking Him for His direction with your new business.
- Thank God for closing all doors that need to be closed and for opening doors that need to be opened in your life.
- Thank God for His grace through this transition period.
- Continue to embrace your new positive associations.
- Continue to formulate your business plan. Start to research your local SCORE office and make contact with the Small Business Administration office which will assist you with your business plan.
- Discuss and brainstorm your business name with your family members and mentor(s).
- Thank God for developing your hearing so you can hear His voice clearly. Spend quiet time with God daily.
- Continue sowing seeds with your talents and offerings.
- Give your tithes (10% of all income you receive).
- Read Psalm 1 and Psalm 91 daily.

Chapter Notes

Chapter To-Do List

Chapter Eight

How to Choose Your Business Location

Location is a key element to the success of your business. When choosing your business location, asking yourself the following questions can alleviate a lot of stress and future problems:

- What is the nature of your business?
- Can you conduct your business from your home legally?
- Can this business be conducted from on-line/Internet/social media?
- Do you need high foot traffic?
- What are the costs for local taxes, utility rates and shopping center fees?
- Is my landlord flexible and cooperative?
- Can I make changes to the building to accommodate my products and services?
- Is it a safe environment for both my customers and my staff?
- Is there anything I need to know about the areas I plan to start my business in? (Always speak with current business owners within the proximity of the area where you are considering starting your business.)

- Visit the location where you plan to start your business during different times of the day, particularly during the morning, noon and late evening. This will give you a more accurate understanding of the environment and the community.
- What is the zoning and signage requirement for that location? Does the zoning permit your type of business at that location?
- What is the proximity to your closest competitors?
- Shop at your closest competitor and observe their service, business volume and their customers. Remember, we are Christian business owners; therefore, we operate with integrity. We are not there to steal customers, we are only there to observe.
- Will your customers have easy access to your business?
- What's the morning and evening traffic flow like? Are you located on the appropriate side of the street to attract traffic flow?
- Does the location fit the nature of your business and the image that your company is trying to create with its customers?

Chapter Assignment

- Exercise at least 40 minutes each day for five days per week.
- Spend quality time with God each day, thanking Him for His direction with your new business.
- Thank God for closing all doors that need to be closed and for opening doors that need to be opened in your life.
- Thank God for His grace through this transition period.
- Thank God for your new positive associations.
- Thank God for giving you the desire to have a prayer partner and mentor in your life.
- Thank God for developing your hearing so you can hear His voice clearly and spend quiet time with Him daily.
- Continue sowing seeds with your talents and offerings. Remember, you cannot out-give God.
- Give your tithes (10% of all income you receive).
- Read Psalm 1 and Psalm 91 daily.

Chapter Notes

Chapter To-Do List

Chapter Nine

Positioning Your Business for Success

Advertizing and Marketing

By now you should have decided on your company name. Research the name you have chosen on your respective state business website. For example, the website for The Department of State Division of Corporations in Florida is www.sunbiz.org. For your respective state, Google the "Department of State" and enter the state where you will operate your business. If you are still having difficulty creating your company name and/or website address, get a family member who is computer savvy to show you how to research company names and website addresses online.

Once you have determined that the name you have chosen is still available, proceed with registering your company name. I recommend that you have an accountant register your company name for you, especially if this is the first business you have registered. If not, carefully complete the necessary documentations discussed in "Registering Your Business." Once you have registered your company name, received confirmation that your new business name is now registered and received your EIN (Federal Employee Identification Number), go to your local city and county tax office. They will inform you about what taxes you need to pay, the frequency you need to pay taxes and if any additional professional licenses are required to operate your business. You will need an EIN to get a checking account from most banks.

Congratulations! You are on your way to becoming a new business owner. Once you have completed the required documentation as determined by law, it's time to proceed with marketing your business.

Creating Your Business Card and Flyer

1. Create you business cards and flyers with easy-to-read fonts. Your business cards and flyers should include:
    i. Your Company Name
    ii. Your Name
    iii. Your Business Address
    iv. Your Business Telephone Number
    v. Your Business Fax Number
    vi. Your Business E-mail Address
    vii. Your Business Website
    viii. Company Logo (Optional)
    ix. Social Media Link (Optional)
2. Tell everyone who will listen to you about your business. They might not be able to use your services but they can refer you to someone who will.
3. Place an ad in your local newspaper business section. This is sometimes free.
4. Send flyers out to businesses/residents within a thirty-mile radius of your business. Speak with your local post office representatives and they will assist you.
5. Find large shopping centers within a five-mile radius of your business and place flyers on vehicles, or distribute flyers to people leaving the major department stores. You should be able to pay a reliable high school student to do this. Make sure you are not breaking your respective city laws with your guerilla marketing efforts.
6. Speak with local school administrators and your church representatives about placing an ad in their bulletin.

7. Attend at least two networking events per week and start to promote your business.
8. Sponsor a charitable event. Make sure the ROI (return on investment) is worth it. Measure the number of attendees and make them among your targeted customers.
9. Join professional organizations which support your specific type of business.
10. Google and research all free local advertising agencies.
11. Ask your banker if you could set up a table in their lobby to promote your **New Business** at least twice a month for the next three months. Your banker would definitely love to see your business flourish so get their input on how they can help you advertise.
12. Research if your community has a local website that you might be able to place it there for free.

Social Media

1. Pay a professional to create a website that represents your company image. Research other websites within your line of business. This will give you a better idea of how you want yours to look.
2. Create a Facebook account. If you are not sure how, give this project to your teenage or young adult children, nieces, nephews or cousins.
3. Creating a Twitter account is another fabulous idea. Make sure you will have the time to blog and keep up with the communications required. Remember, this is a reflection on your business so you need to maintain the image you are trying to portray.
4. Attend a social media workshop, especially one that is presented by your local SBA (Small Business

Administration), SCORE or chamber office. These classes are usually free or very affordable.

Chapter Assignment

- Exercise at least 45 minutes each day for four days per week.
- Spend quality time with God each day, thanking Him for His direction with your new business.
- Create your business card and flyers.
- Create a social media page according to business image you desire to portray.
- Thank God for closing all doors that need to be closed and for opening doors that need to be opened in your life.
- Thank God for His grace through this transition period.
- Thank God for your new positive associations.
- Thank God for giving you the desire to have a prayer partner and mentor in your life.
- Continue to formulate your business plan.
- Research local chambers of commerce and schedule your first networking event. At this point, you are attending only to observe.
- Research the company name you have chosen on your local business administration website. Recommendation: Seek an accountant's assistance when registering your business name.

- Thank God for developing your hearing so you can hear His voice clearly.
- Continue sowing seeds with your talents and offerings.
- Give your tithes (10% of all earnings you receive).
- Read Psalm 1 and Psalm 91 daily.

Chapter Notes

Chapter To-Do List

Chapter Ten

Selecting a Successful Team

Congratulations, your business is flourishing and now you need to hire some good help. Listed below are some guidelines to follow so you can reduce staffing costs and at the same time, maintain a productive staff.

Making the Right Hiring Decisions

Here are some pointers to consider when hiring your staff:

- Determine the type of help you need.
- Determine the required experience this person should have.
- How many hours will he or she have to work per day and per week?
- Do you have or project to have funds available to cover payroll expenses for your employees?
- Once you have determined that you truly need additional help, then move forward by advertising your need for help.

Now you are ready to proceed with interviewing potential candidates:

- Schedule quality time (at least one hour of uninterrupted time) to interview candidates.
- Have all applicants complete an employment application. Create an application for your use.

There are free employment applications online. You can check with your local Department of Labor or Workforce Office to see if your application meets state and federal government standards.

- Employment applications should include an "At will" clause that states either party can terminate the employment contract or agreement at will and with no liability.
- Have at least one other person you trust interview the candidate independently. If it is a management position, have at least three interviewers.
- Record answers to your questions during your interviews.
- Have no distractions during interviews (i.e. phone calls.)
- Ask open-ended questions (questions that require more than a yes or no answer).
- Listen for previous employment behavior and consider them to be future behaviors.
- Pay attention to body language. The candidate should be able to look you in the eyes when responding to your questions. If he or she fails to do so, chances are that the candidate is not telling the truth or is possibly hiding something. Some cultures do not make direct eye contact with superiors; consider this before rejecting the candidate.
- Listen for team-player clues.

- Evaluate the most qualified person versus the most suitable person for a position. Are you willing to hire someone that has all the required credentials and no work history, versus someone who has the proven work history and no credentials?

- Adhere to established hiring practices and be consistent with all applicants. Do not show favoritism (this can protect you from potential lawsuit).

- Always check a minimum of three references.

- Consistency with employees minimizes discrimination lawsuits. If you conduct background checks and require drug testing, do the same for all employees. Check with your state for up-to-date labor laws.

- Have an established wage scale and be consistent with all employees.

Maintaining Your Workforce:

- Orientate your new hires with their job responsibilities. This should take place prior to putting your new team members to work. During orientation, you should also talk with your new team members regarding your business:
    - History
    - Vision
    - Mission
    - Company Policies
        - Dress Code

        - Probationary Period
        - Pay Period (weekly or bi-weekly); verify your state law requirement
        - Progressive Discipline
        - Holiday Pay
        - Tardiness
        - Misconduct
        - Solicitation
        - Harassment
        - Vacation Pay
        - Associate Incentives
    - Who are your customers?
    - What is great customer service for your business?
    - How do you keep your customers coming back and how does it correlate to his or her wages?
    - Explain the more profit/more job security concept.
- Have an established employee recognition program in place. You can start by awarding your team members who have gone over and beyond the call of duty with a small token of appreciation. This is not to be mistaken with an employee who just simply does their job.
- Celebrate success and communicate failure.
- Solicit your employees' ideas and keep a system in place to show that you have implemented or plan to implement their ideas, or explain why it might not be the appropriate time to implement the idea. Be positive when communicating this so that your team

members will not lose interest in participating in this program.

- Compliment employees in public and discipline them behind closed doors.
- Invest in your employees by giving them health benefits and education reimbursement whenever you can afford to do so. The ROI will be worth it.
- Get to know your employees.
- Be a positive role model to your employees and respect them. When they speak with you confidentially, let it remain that way. Do not tell their business to other team members; you will lose their trust.

Employer Responsibility:
(Always verify with your local Labor Office, Federal and state Labor Laws for up to date information)

- Maintain accurate employee eligibility information for working in the US. Always check with your local Workforce Office for any changes with the eligibility information documentation process. You will need to complete and turn in accurate documentation within three days from the date of hire.

- Maintain a safe working environment for yourself and your employees.

- Communicate with your employees regarding their pay period (weekly/bi-weekly/monthly).

- Complete Federal Income Tax Withholdings Documentation. Consult your local government for any additional documentation that needs to be completed by you and your employees.

- Treat all employees fairly. Be consistent with your policies and procedures.
- Know your state laws regarding Workers Compensation, Labor Laws and Payroll.
- Allow your new team members to be mentored by someone on your team.

Chapter Assignment

- Exercise at least 45 minutes each day for four days per week.
- Spend quality time with God each day, thanking Him for His direction with your new business.
- Thank God for His grace through this transition period.
- Select a mentor and a prayer partner. Do not be in a rush to do so if your spirit doesn't lead you.
- Attend a networking event (at this point, you should already be promoting your business).
- Continue to formulate your business plan. Reminder: It's ok to update it at least twice per year.
- Congratulations, you have now selected a company name for your business.
- Research all the companies in your city that promote businesses for free.
- Thank God for developing your hearing so you can hear His voice clearly. Spend quiet time with God daily.
- Continue sowing seeds with your talents and offerings.
- Give your tithes (10% of all earnings you receive).
- Read Psalm 1 and Psalm 91 daily.

Chapter Notes

Chapter To-Do List

Chapter Eleven

Your Business Startup Expenses

Accounting

Complete the following which will give you a true picture of what you need to start your business. Some areas may not apply to your respective business:

Startup Expenses

Basis of Capital

Owners' Investment

Your name and percent of ownership	$ -
Other investor	-
Other investor	-

Other investor	-
Total Investment	$ -

Bank Loans

Bank	$ -
Total Bank Loans	$ -

Other Loans

Source	$ -
Total Other Loans	$ -

Startup Expenses

Real Estate/Building

Construction	$

	-
Purchases	-
Remodeling	-
Other	-
Total	$ -

Leasehold Improvements

Item 1	$ -
Item 2	-
Item 3	-
Item 4	-
Total	$ -

Capital Equipment List

	$
Furniture	-
Equipment	-
Fixtures	-
Machinery	-
Other	-
	$
Total	-

Location and Admin. Expenses

	$
Rental Equipment	-
Utility deposits	-
Legal and accounting fees	-
Prepaid insurance	

	-
Pre-opening salaries	-
Other	-
Total	$ -

Opening Inventory

Stage 1	$ -
Stage 2	-
Stage 3	-
Stage 4	-
Stage 5	-
Total Inventory	$ -

Advertising and

Marketing Expenses

	$
Advertising	-
Signage	-
Printing	-
Other/additional signage	-
Total	$ -

Other Expenses

	$
Other expense	-
Other expense	-
Total	$ -

$ -

Working Capital	$ -

Summary Statement

Sources of Capital

Owner's and other investments	$ -
Bank loans	-
Other loans	-
Total Source of Funds	$ -

Startup Expenses

Buildings/real estate	$ -
Leasehold improvements	-
Capital equipment	-

Location/administration expenses	-
Opening inventory	-
Advertising/marketing expenses	-
Other expenses	-
Working capital	-
Total Startup Expenses	$ -

Security for Loan Proposal

Security for Loans	**Value**	**Description**
Real estate	$ -	
Other Security	-	
Other Security		

-

Other Security -

Owners

Your name here

Other owner

Other owner

Other owner

Other Loan Guarantors

Loan guarantor 1

Loan guarantor 2

Loan guarantor 3

Chapter Assignment

- Exercise at least one hour each day for four days per week.
- Spend quality time with God each day, thanking Him for His divine favor and divine connections for your new business.
- Begin to work on your Start-up Expense Worksheet
- Edit your flyers and business cards in preparation for your upcoming networking event and new business day celebration.
- Thank God for His grace through this transition period.
- Select a mentor and a prayer partner. If you are not comfortable with anyone you know, continue to praise God for one anyways. Do not rush this process.
- Attend at least two networking events per month. Always pray for divine connections and favor from God before you attend these events.
- Continue to formulate your business plan. Have a professional a representative from your local SCORE or SBA (Small Business Administration) office to review your business plan.
- Think about members in your family, church and community who you might be able to employ in your business. Pray to God for guidance through this process.
- Research all the companies in your city that promote businesses for free and promote your business with the reputable companies.

- Thank God for speaking to you and submit yourself to His will.
- Continue sowing seeds with your talents and offerings.
- Give your tithes (10% of all income you receive).
- Read Psalm 1 and Psalm 91 daily.

Chapter Notes:

Chapter To-Do List:

Chapter Twelve

Successful Networking

In order to build a successful business, you need a great customer/client base. Since your business is new and you are trying to build your customer base, I would recommend that you attend at least one to two networking events per week. Be more concerned about building a business relationship rather than just handing out business cards. Remember, a recommendation is always better than a referral. People recommend who they know and give a personal character reference. It is also a good idea to volunteer your time with charitable organizations because in order to reap a harvest, you have to sow seeds first. As you volunteer among these people, you are building a business relationship with them.

Getting Prepared for a Networking Event:

Some of what is mentioned in this chapter might just be common sense to you, but you would be surprise to see how often these are overlooked.

- Proper hygiene is important. You want your space to be welcoming. No overpowering cologne or perfume.
- Wear a dark-colored suit (black, brown or dark blue). Note: You do not want your clothes to be a distraction; instead, you want people to pay attention to what you have to say. You want them to remember your business services, not what you were wearing.

- Invest in a name badge. It looks more professional. Your name badge should have your name and your company name. Your name badge should be worn on the top right of your jacket for easy visibility.
- Makeup should be worn in moderation; again, don't wear anything that will be a distraction.
- Women - no purses. Wear a suit with pockets to keep your business cards on hand. Keep all business cards you receive as your beginning network base. Develop a system of putting all business cards you receive from others in your left pocket and keep your business cards in your right pocket. This way you will not accidently give away someone's business card while thinking it was your own.
- Remember to use a firm hand shake and maintain good eye contact because this will validate that you are a strong and serious business owner.
- Take notes on business cards.
- "Divide and conquer!" If you attend a networking event with your spouse or child, each of you should work the room independently. This will give you the opportunity to meet more potential clients/customers.
- Spend five minutes max with each prospect. Reminder, this is not a social gathering; it is about business.
- Know your "Elevator Speech." This is precise, well-rehearsed description of your product and/or service. The "Elevator Speech" concept proposes that anyone should be able to understand your business in the time it would take to ride an elevator one floor.

Reminder: The best way to sell is not to sell. It is always good to build a business relationship first, because a recommendation is better than a referral.

Chapter Assignment

- Exercise at least 30 minutes each day for three days per week.
- Spend quality time with God each day, thanking Him for His direction with your new business.
- Send a thank you e-mail to everyone you have met at this event that you have a business interest in.
- Thank God for closing all doors that need to be closed and for opening doors that need to be opened in your life.
- Thank God for His grace through the transition period.
- Select a prayer partner and a mentor according to God's will and purpose for your life.
- Continue to formulate your business plan.
- Attend at least two networking events per month. Always pray for divine connections and favor from God before you attend any event.
- Continue to advertize and promote your business/ministry.
- Thank God for speaking to you.
- Submit to the will of God for you ministry/business.
- Continue sowing seeds with your talents and offerings.

- Give your tithes (10% of all income you receive).
- Read Psalm 1 and Psalm 91 daily.

Chapter Notes

Chapter To-Do List

Summary Chapter

Stay Encouraged

Now that you have started your business/ministry or career, here are some reminders of which you should never lose focus.

You **must** have a personal relationship with God through:

Prayer

Fasting

Praise and worshiping

Reading the word of God

Meditating on God's word

Spending quiet, uninterrupted time alone

Spending quiet, uninterrupted time with God

Each day, pray and ask God for your assignment that day and ask Him to help you not to miss your visitations and divine appointments from Him

Celebrate your milestone achievements

You **must** sow seeds:

Your time

Your finances

Your talents

Introduce this ministry (God Wills Ministry) to at least two people who need to start their own business/ministry

As you climb the ladder of success, become a mentor to someone else (pass the torch)

You **must** stay faithful:

As you wait for your breakthrough, volunteer your time at charitable organizations near your area

Form a Prayer Warrior Team (PWT) for yourself. This is a list of at least two people you can call anytime to pray, fast and intercede with you. These people should be more like your spiritual confidants. You should be able to share your unedited feelings with them.

Build Your Network Group

Reminder: Christians are not the only people who do business; however, never compromise your faith for a dollar. Expand your business circle.

Get involved with local chambers and charitable organizations.

Allow yourself to be in the presence of positive people and successful business owners.

Attend at least two networking events per week.

Stay connected with me, your mentor, prayer partner and prayer warrior.

Create a monthly support group for Kingdom business owners.

As you have now gone through valleys and experienced what it means to trust in God. I am sure at this point that you have several testimonies. Yes, you went through a test so you could have a testimony. Now you can be a witness to how great God is. This is your season to soar, to see the manifestation of your harvest. Stay focused and **always** remember that God's grace is on your life. Be sure to share your testimony with others so they can be helped. God blesses us to be a blessing to others, so remember to share the wealth.

As you continue to maintain an excellent relationship with your loyal customers, do not become complacent with their loyalty. Always seek new ways to motivate them. Have incentive programs in place for them, just as you would your new customers.

I believe the process of starting your business is much like being a pregnant woman. During the first trimester, the pregnant woman goes through the phase of what we call "morning sickness." She is nauseous, yet excited. In the same way, aspiring business owners during their first couple of months in business become very anxious and nervous all at once. They sometimes ask themselves, "Am I doing the right thing?" Both the pregnant woman and the aspiring business owner continue to plan for that big day when they will give birth. The business owner will give birth to a new business while the pregnant woman will give birth to a child. Both will go through the exciting stage, one buying clothes for her newborn the other selecting a business name for his or her new business and sharing the idea of opening a new business; both are so excited and happy.

As the birthing stage draws near, both the pregnant woman and the aspiring business owner start to feel tension. In both cases, the tension stems from something within them that needs to give birth or come forth. The pregnant woman can touch her stomach and feel the baby inside her. She talks to it and comforts it. The aspiring business owner has God to speak to confirming that he or she knows that God will help them to birth their new ideas. This is where faith can separate the two. The pregnant woman has not seen what's inside of her but she trusts her doctor that it's a baby. Therefore, she treats her pregnancy as if she is carrying a human being in her womb. How much more should we trust God that whatever He has impregnated us with, we will also give birth?

When a pregnant woman goes into labor, she pushes her way through the pain. The first stage might include contractions that are thirty minutes apart. Because she has already prepared herself for this moment, she knows what breathing technique to use to relieve her pain. As the contractions get closer she knows to push harder and longer. At no point does she ever quit. She knows something is inside of her that needs to be birthed. As she pushes through the pain with her mother on her left and her husband on her right, she knows that she still has to do the work. The tougher the pain, the harder she knows she has to push.

On the other hand, there's an aspiring business owner who starts to feel challenged. This might be due to the stress of getting all the required permits passed for the new building or not being able to get approval for the loan they need to buy the necessary equipment for the store. It might be that the owner has not been able to find the perfect location for the business, and it is at this stage that the aspiring business owner may become weary and start to question himself/herself by thinking, "Am I doing the right thing?" This is where most aspiring business owners fail or quit. They don't push themselves like the woman in labor would. They just throw in the towel or even let their dream fade away. Don't you know it's the plan of the devil to put up road blocks just as you are about to cross the finish line of one level that would then transcend you into another level? Just as a woman in labor pushes her way through the pain, so should you. The stronger the pain, the harder you should Push! Push! Push! If you feel you can't push anymore, bring out all your weapons; it's war time and God is with you so you will conquer in Jesus' name.

1. Our bible has a verse for all situations. Speak God's word over your situation. "No weapon formed against me shall prosper (Protection Scripture)." "Through God all things are possible (Scripture of faith)." "I am the lender and not the borrower (Scripture of prosperity)." "I live by faith, and not by sight (Scripture of faith)." "By Your favor, Lord, You have established me a strong mountain Scripture of favor)." Speak God's word until they come alive.
2. Call your prayer warrior and unite with him or her through prayer and fasting.
3. Never give up on God's will for your life.

Your challenges build your experience pool which turns you into an expert in your field. So embrace your setbacks and consider them to be your downtime for better preparation. Use them as your steps to another level of greatness. When you have done everything you are supposed to do, be still and trust God. His timing is not our timing. He is always on time. God is never late. Always believe His word. He never lies. His word is final. You will be successful if you trust God.

Be reminded that:

- Your blessings are dependent on your willingness to push through your struggles.

- A family that prays together stays together. Have prayer time with your family.

- Satan attacks those in line for a blessing. Your attack is usually because of the blessings in front of you. The attack is supposed to detour you and keep distracted. But if you are in relationship with God, He will warn you before you encounter it; may be through dreams, visions, a prophet, your spiritual leader, or while communing with Him. There is no limit as to how God will communicate with us; pray for a stronger spirit of discernment so you will not miss when He is speaking to you. Sometimes situations we go through are a part of our process for God's will to manifest in our life. Nothing will happen to us unless God allows it. If God allows it, it will be use for His glory. Remember, Jesus warned Peter that Satan has asked to sift all of him as wheat (Luke 22:31). Satan has to get permission from God to touch us, so know that everything happening in your life will ultimately be used to glorify God. Yes, sometimes we allow access by sinning.

- Pray for what you want versus what you don't want. You will magnify what you focus on in your life. Focus on the positive.

- Speak blessings over yourself and your family everyday. Life and death is in your mouth. Create positive things with your mouth.

- STOP COMPLAINING! Instead ask God what are you suppose to learn from the situations or challenges you are encountering.

- Every situation is God-used but not God-sent. Your situation will be used to develop you. It's training ground. The quicker you pass the test, the faster your promotion will come. Remember, when the student is taking a test, the teacher is quiet. If you believe God is not responding to you and you are living right, chances are that you are taking a test. Praise and worship Him with the tears in your eyes, knowing that this season will pass. "Only salvation is lasting."

- Success is in your differences and your uniqueness. Love yourself. Look in the mirror each morning and say something positive to yourself; stop waiting on people to speak positive things in your life.

- Luke 6:38 [38]Give, and it shall be given unto you; good measure, pressed down, and shaken together, and running over, shall men give into your bosom. For with the same measure that ye mete withal it shall be measured to you. Sow financial seed. The seasons of your life will change every time you decide to use your faith.

- The seed you sow is the seed you will reap bountifully. Do well unto others on purpose.

- Be respectful and obedient to your leaders.

- What you feed grows and what you starve dies. Feed your relationship with God.

- How long did you spend with your family today? Have you told them and show them that you love them?

- How long did you spend gossiping or on social media today? Make sure you spend more time with God.

- How long did you spend praying and worshiping God today? Have you told God lately that you love Him? Have you told Him thanks for the air you breathe? Have you told Him thanks that you can walk, eat, see and talk?

- How long did you spend watching TV today?

Invest in your mind, your family, future and most importantly, your relationship with God and you will have a prosperous life.

<u>My Personal Daily Declaration for you to say Daily</u>

<u>Father God, forgive me for all my sins (Read and Pray Psalm 51)</u>

<u>Job 22:28 - I shall decree a thing and it shall be established in my life</u>

1. I will hearken diligently unto the voice of the LORD my God, to observe and to do all His commandments which He command me this day, that the LORD my God will set me on high above all nations of the earth.

2. I will be a blessing to someone today and today, someone will be a blessing to me and my family.

3. I am a mighty woman of God and this is my set time for favor.

4. The Lord will release angels to war against any spirit assigned to block my prayers from being answered.

5. The floodgates of heaven are open over my family and my life and we will have supernatural experiences today.

6. I will cooperate with God at all times.

7. I am chosen by God and He is hovering over me.

8. I am a good steward to the dreams and visions that God has given.

9. I will hearken unto the voice of the Lord my God at all times.

10. I am blessed in the city, blessed in the field, blessed in my basket, blessed in my store and every area of my life.

11. I have knowledge, wisdom and favor from God and I will live His will for my life.

12. My leaders are blessed and anointed to lead me and no weapon formed against them and their family will prosper.

13. I am blessed coming in and blessed going out.

14. The Lord shall cause my enemies that rise up against me to be smitten before my face: they shall come out against me one way, and flee before me seven ways.

15. The Lord will command His blessing upon me, and everything that my hand touches will be a blessing.

16. I will bless the Lord at all times. His praises shall continually be in my mouth.

17. I have favor with God and man today and all the days of my life.

18. My family and I will serve the Lord. We will live God's will for our lives.

19. No evil shall befall my family and me. No plague shall come near our dwelling.

20. I have favor with God and man. My family and I have perfect health.

21. I overcome evil with good.

22. God gives me knowledge and wisdom in all areas where I lack.

23. I will always speak positive things over my life and my children's life.

24. My bloodline is blessed and no curses dwell within.

25. The Lord's right hand is on my family and I at all times.

26. I will not miss any visitations from You, Lord.

27. All people of the earth shall see that I am called by the name of the Lord.

28. The Lord shall make me plenteous in goods, in the fruit of my body, and in the fruit of my business/job, and in the fruit of my children, in the land which the LORD has given me.

29. I will lend unto many nations, and I will not borrow.

30. I am the head, and not the tail. I am above, not beneath.

31. I will speak and teach with the fire of God on my tongue.

32. I am baptized with the Holy Ghost and fire of God.

33. I have knowledge, wisdom and favor from God to do His work.

34. I am a servant of God, I am called in Christ, I have liberty in Christ. I have boldness and access in Christ.

35. I can do all things through Christ who strengthens me. I have the mind and love of Christ.

36. I dwell in the secret place of the Most High, and I abide under the shadow of the Almighty.

37. All nations and generations call me blessed.

38. I am chosen by God and I am blessed. God is choosing for my family and I today.

39. Angels have been dispatched by God to work on my family's behalf and my behalf.

40. My family and I will have a Matthew 6 "Kingdom Experience" today.

41. I am rooted and grounded in the love of Jesus.

42. This is the best day of my life and my day will end perfectly according to God's will for my life.

43. God, I receive every seed you have to planted in my life. God is shining His light on my situation.

44. My eyes are anointed to **SEE ONLY** what the Lord wants me to see.

45. My ears are anointed to HEAR **ONLY** what the Lord wants me to hear.

46. My lips are anointed to **SPEAK ONLY** what the Lord wants me to speak.

47. My spiritual discernment is operating as God intended for it to operate.

48. Everyone who comes around me leaves as a better person.

49. God is giving me fresh eyes to see opportunities today.

50. God is giving me fresh ideas today and I will put into practice every idea He has downloaded today.

51. I am blessed with all spiritual blessings in heavenly places in Christ Jesus.

52. I will complete all assignments God has for me today.

53. I call forth favor from the east, west, north and south.

54. I am prosperous in all areas of my life.

55. God is blessing Jerusalem (Psalm 122:6; Genesis 12:3). **THANK YOU, JESUS.**

Blessings Prayer From Me toYou

May God's best come upon you and overtake you as you hear and obey the word and voice of God. I speak that peace and strength would rise up in your emotions, for God has **not** given you the spirit of fear but of power, love and a sound mind. May your spirit and your heart seek after the perfect will of God.

Be blessed in your home. Be blessed in your businesses. Be blessed in you ministries. Be blessed in your career and in all areas of your life.

Be quick to forgive one another. Let rest and renewal be yours as you refuse to let the sun go down on your wrath.

Your obedience to tithing and offering will ensure that your businesses and place of labor will yield greater increase. All you lay your hands upon will flourish. You are blessed and highly favored. You are the head and not the tail. You are the lender and not the borrower.

You shall overcome the devil. No weapons formed against you shall prosper. The Holy Spirit will order your steps away from evil and He will deliver you from temptation. Your enemies that rise up before you shall flee before you seven ways. I release God's angels to go with you, keep you and to watch over you and your loved ones.

May the Lord bless you and keep you and cause His face to shine upon you. I bless you in the mighty name of Jesus. Amen!!!

Now go and be who God has created you to be!!!

My Time Spent Per 24 Hours Exercise

Reminder: Whatever you spent your time doing will manifest in your life.

	TV/ Internet	Family/ Work	Self / Exercise	Praying/ Meditating on God Word	Sleep	
Monday	2 hours/3 hours	1 hours /11 hours	30 minutes/ 20 minutes	10 minutes	6 hours	24 Hours
Tuesday						24 Hours
Wednesday						24 Hours
Thursday						24 Hours
Friday						24 Hours
Saturday						24 Hours
Sunday						24 Hours

Chapter Notes

Chapter To-Do List

Book Contact

Janet Melwani

PO Box 691966

Orlando, FL 32869

(321) 305-0358

Janetmelwani@yahoo.com

www.Godwills.com

Please include any testimonies or insight you received from this book.

Contact us at the listed informations for conferences and workshops.

www.ingramcontent.com/pod-product-compliance
Lightning Source LLC
Chambersburg PA
CBHW051906170526
45168CB00001B/262
9781517588618